POEMS

OF

HOME AND TRAVEL.

BY

BAYARD TAYLOR.

BOSTON:
TICKNOR AND FIELDS.
M DCCC LV.

STEREOTYPED AT THE
BOSTON STEREOTYPE FOUNDRY.

New editions of the " Rhymes of Travel," (published in 1849,) and the "Book of Romances, Lyrics, and Songs," (published in 1851,) having been called for, the author has carefully revised both works, rejecting much that did not appear worthy of republication, and now offers them again to the public, together with a number of new poems, written since the appearance of his "Poems of the Orient." The two volumes, therefore, contain all the poetry which he is willing to acknowledge, up to the present time. He desires a speedy forgetfulness for what he has omitted.

New York, *October*, 1855.

TO

GEORGE H. BOKER.

To you the homage of this book I bring.
    The earliest and the latest flowers I yield,
    And though their hues betray a barren field,
I know you will not slight the offering.
You were the mate of my poetic spring;
    To you its buds of little worth concealed
    More than the summer years have since revealed,
Or doubtful autumn from the stem shall fling.
    But here they are, the buds, the blossoms blown;
If rich or scant, the wreath is at your feet;
    And though it were the freshest ever grown,
To you its incense could not be more sweet,
    Since with it goes a love to match your own,
A heart, dear Friend, that never falsely beat.

CONTENTS.

ROMANCES AND LYRICS.

PAGE

Metempsychosis of the Pine, ... 11

Hylas, ... 18

Kubleh: a Story of the Assyrian Desert, . . . 25

Love and Solitude, ... 32

Mon-da-Min; or, The Romance of Maize, . . . 43

The Soldier and the Pard, ... 60

Ariel in the cloven Pine, ... 71

The Harp: an Ode, ... 76

Serapion, ... 80

"Moan, ye wild Winds!" 85

Taurus, ... 87

The Odalisque, ... 91

Sorrowful Music, ... 93

The Tulip-Tree, ... 95

Autumnal Vespers, ... 98

Ode to Shelley, ... 101

Sicilian Wine, ... 104
Summer's Bacchanal, ... 109
Storm-Lines, ... 112
The Two Visions, ... 115
The Life of Earth, ... 117
Storm Song, ... 120
Song, ... 122
The Waves, ... 123
Song, ... 126
Cricket Song, ... 127
Wordsworth, ... 129
Sonnet. To G. H. B., ... 130

CALIFORNIAN BALLADS AND POEMS.

Manuela, ... 133
The Fight of Paso del Mar, ... 138
The Pine Forest of Monterey, ... 142
El Canelo, ... 147
The Eagle Hunter, ... 151
The Summer Camp, ... 154
The Bison Track, ... 162

RHYMES OF TRAVEL, AND EARLY POEMS.

The Tomb of Charlemagne, ... 169
The Wayside Dream, ... 172
Steyermark, ... 176

To a Bavarian Girl, ... 178
In Italy, ... 180
The Statue in the Snow, ... 182
The dearest Image, ... 185
A Bacchic Ode, ... 187
A Funeral Thought, ... 190
The Angel of the Soul, ... 193
An Hour, ... 197
The Norseman's Ride, ... 201
The Voice of the Fire, ... 204
A Requiem in the North, ... 207
A Voice from Piedmont, ... 210
The Continents, ... 213
The Mountains, ... 218
Life, . —. 219
L'Envoi, ... 220

LATER POEMS.

Wind and Sea, ... 225
My Dead, ... 227
The Lost Crown, ... 229
Studies for Pictures:
I. — At Home, ... 232
II. — The Neighbor, ... 233
III. — Under the Stars, ... 235
IV. — In the Morning, ... 237

Sunken Treasures, ... 240

A Fantasy, ... 243

The Voyagers, ... 246

Memory, ... 248

The Mariners, ... 250

Note, ... 253

ROMANCES AND LYRICS.

METEMPSYCHOSIS OF THE PINE.

As when the haze of some wan moonlight makes
  Familiar fields a land of mystery,
Where all is changed, and some new presence wakes
    In flower, and bush, and tree,—

Another life the life of Day o'erwhelms;
  The Past from present consciousness takes hue,
And we remember vast and cloudy realms
    Our feet have wandered through:

So, oft, some moonlight of the mind makes dumb
  The stir of outer thought: wide open seems
The gate wherethrough strange sympathies have come,
    The secret of our dreams;

The source of fine impressions, shooting deep
  Below the failing plummet of the sense;
Which strike beyond all Time, and backward sweep
      Through all intelligence.

We touch the lower life of beast and clod,
  And the long process of the ages see
From blind old Chaos, ere the breath of God
      Moved it to harmony.

All outward wisdom yields to that within,
  Whereof nor creed nor canon holds the key;
We only feel that we have ever been,
      And evermore shall be.

And thus I know, by memories unfurled
  In rarer moods, and many a nameless sign,
That once in Time, and somewhere in the world,
      I was a towering Pine,

Rooted upon a cape that overhung
  The entrance to a mountain gorge; whereon
The wintry shadow of a peak was flung,
      Long after rise of sun.

Behind, the silent snows; and wide below,
  The rounded hills made level, lessening down
To where a river washed with sluggish flow
    A many-templed town.

There did I clutch the granite with firm feet,
  There shake my boughs above the roaring gulf,
When mountain whirlwinds through the passes beat,
    And howled the mountain wolf.

There did I louder sing than all the floods
  Whirled in white foam adown the precipice,
And the sharp sleet that stung the naked woods
    Answer with sullen hiss:

But when the peaceful clouds rose white and high
  On blandest airs that April skies could bring,
Through all my fibres thrilled the tender sigh,
    The sweet unrest of Spring.

She, with warm fingers laced in mine, did melt
  In fragrant balsam my reluctant blood;
And with a smart of keen delight I felt
    The sap in every bud,

And tingled through my rough old bark, and fast
  Pushed out the younger green, that smoothed my tones,
When last year's needles to the wind I cast,
    And shed my scaly cones.

I held the eagle till the mountain mist
  Rolled from the azure paths he came to soar,
And like a hunter, on my gnarled wrist
    The dappled falcon bore.

Poised o'er the blue abyss, the morning lark
  Sang, wheeling near in rapturous carouse;
And hart and hind, soft-pacing through the dark,
    Slept underneath my boughs.

Down on the pasture-slopes the herdsman lay,
  And for the flock his birchen trumpet blew;
There ruddy children tumbled in their play,
    And lovers came to woo.

And once an army, crowned with triumph, came
  Out of the hollow bosom of the gorge,
With mighty banners in the wind aflame,
    Borne on a glittering surge

Of tossing spears, a flood that homeward rolled,
  While cymbals timed their steps of victory,
And horn and clarion from their throats of gold
        Sang with a savage glee.

I felt the mountain walls below me shake,
  Vibrant with sound, and through my branches poured
The glorious gust: my song thereto did make
        Magnificent accord.

Some blind harmonic instinct pierced the rind
  Of that slow life which made me straight and high,
And I became a harp for every wind,
        A voice for every sky;

When fierce autumnal gales began to blow,
  Roaring all day in concert, hoarse and deep;
And then made silent with my weight of snow—
        A spectre on the steep;

Filled with a whispering gush, like that which flows
  Through organ-stops, when sank the sun's red disk
Beyond the city, and in blackness rose
        Temple and obelisk;

Or breathing soft, as one who sighs in prayer,
Mysterious sounds of portent and of might,
What time I felt the wandering waves of air
Pulsating through the night.

And thus for centuries my rhythmic chant
Rolled down the gorge, or surged about the hill:
Gentle, or stern, or sad, or jubilant,
At every season's will.

No longer Memory whispers whence arose
The doom that tore me from my place of pride:
Whether the storms that load the peak with snows,
And start the mountain slide,

Let fall a fiery bolt to smite my top,
Upwrenched my roots, and o'er the precipice
Hurled me, a dangling wreck, erelong to drop
Into the wild abyss;

Or whether hands of men, with scornful strength
And force from Nature's rugged armory lent,
Sawed through my heart and rolled my tumbling length
Sheer down the steep descent.

All sense departed, with the boughs I wore;
  And though I moved with mighty gales at strife,
A mast upon the seas, I sang no more,
    And music was my life.

Yet still that life awakens, brings again
  Its airy anthems, resonant and long,
Till Earth and Sky, transfigured, fill my brain
    With rhythmic sweeps of song.

Thence am I made a poet: thence are sprung
  Those motions of the soul, that sometimes reach
Beyond all grasp of Art, — for which the tongue
    Is ignorant of speech.

And if some wild, full-gathered harmony
  Roll its unbroken music through my line,
There lives and murmurs, faintly though it be,
    The Spirit of the Pine.

HYLAS.

Storm-wearied Argo slept upon the water.
No cloud was seen; on blue and craggy Ida
The hot noon lay, and on the plain's enamel;
Cool, in his bed, alone, the swift Scamander.
"Why should I haste?" said young and rosy Hylas:
"The seas were rough, and long the way from Colchis.
Beneath the snow-white awning slumbers Jason,
Pillowed upon his tame Thessalian panther;
The shields are piled, the listless oars suspended
On the black thwarts, and all the hairy bondsmen
Doze on the benches. They may wait for water,
Till I have bathed in mountain-born Scamander."

So said, unfilleting his purple chlamys,
And putting down his urn, he stood a moment,
Breathing the faint, warm odor of the blossoms
That spangled thick the lovely Dardan meadows.

Then, stooping lightly, loosened he his buskins,
And felt with shrinking feet the crispy verdure,
Naked, save one light robe that from his shoulder
Hung to his knee, the youthful flush revealing
Of warm, white limbs, half-nerved with coming manhood,
Yet fair and smooth with tenderness of beauty.
Now to the river's sandy marge advancing,
He dropped the robe, and raised his head exulting
In the clear sunshine, that with beam embracing
Held him against Apollo's glowing bosom.
For sacred to Latona's son is Beauty,
Sacred is Youth, the joy of youthful feeling.
A joy indeed, a living joy, was Hylas,
Whence Jove-begotten Hêraclês, the mighty,
To men though terrible, to him was gentle
Smoothing his rugged nature into laughter
When the boy stole his club, or from his shoulders
Dragged the huge paws of the Nemæan lion.

The thick, brown locks, tossed backward from his forehead,
Fell soft about his temples; manhood's blossom
Not yet had sprouted on his chin, but freshly
Curved the fair cheek, and full the red lips' parting,
Like a loose bow, that just has launched its arrow.

His large blue eyes, with joy dilate and beamy,
Were clear as the unshadowed Grecian heaven;
Dewy and sleek his dimpled shoulders rounded
To the white arms and whiter breast between them.
Downward, the supple lines had less of softness:
His back was like a god's; his loins were moulded
As if some pulse of power began to waken;
The springy fulness of his thighs, outswerving,
Sloped to his knee, and, lightly dropping downward,
Drew the curved lines that breathe, in rest, of motion.

He saw his glorious limbs reversely mirrored
In the still wave, and stretched his foot to press it
On the smooth sole that answered at the surface:
Alas! the shape dissolved in glimmering fragments.
Then, timidly at first, he dipped, and catching
Quick breath, with tingling shudder, as the waters
Swirled round his thighs, and deeper, slowly deeper,
Till on his breast the River's cheek was pillowed,
And deeper still, till every shoreward ripple
Talked in his ear, and like a cygnet's bosom
His white, round shoulder shed the dripping crystal.
There, as he floated, with a rapturous motion,
The lucid coolness folding close around him,
The lily-cradling ripples murmured, "Hylas!"
He shook from off his ears the hyacinthine

Curls, that nad lain unwet upon the water,
And still the ripples murmured, "Hylas! Hylas!"
He thought: "The voices are but ear-born music.
Pan dwells not here, and Echo still is calling
From some high cliff that tops a Thracian valley:
So long mine ears, on tumbling Hellespontus,
Have heard the sea waves hammer Argo's forehead,
That I misdeem the fluting of this current
For some lost nymph —" Again the murmur, "Hylas!"
And with the sound a cold, smooth arm around him
Slid like a wave, and down the clear, green darkness
Glimmered on either side a shining bosom, —
Glimmered, uprising slow; and ever closer
Wound the cold arms, till, climbing to his shoulders,
Their cheeks lay nestled, while the purple tangles,
Their loose hair made, in silken mesh enwound him.
Their eyes of clear, pale emerald then uplifting,
They kissed his neck with lips of humid coral,
And once again there came a murmur, "Hylas!
O, come with us! O, follow where we wander
Deep down beneath the green, translucent ceiling, —
Where on the sandy bed of old Scamander
With cool white buds we braid our purple tresses,
Lulled by the bubbling waves around us stealing!
Thou fair Greek boy, O, come with us! O, follow

Where thou no more shalt hear Propontis riot,
But by our arms be lapped in endless quiet,
Within the glimmering caves of Ocean hollow!
We have no love; alone, of all the Immortals,
We have no love. O, love us, we who press thee
With faithful arms, though cold, — whose lips caress
thee, —
Who hold thy beauty prisoned! Love us, Hylas!"
The sound dissolved in liquid murmurs, calling
Still as it faded, "Come with us, O, follow!"

The boy grew chill to feel their twining pressure
Lock round his limbs, and bear him, vainly striving,
Down from the noonday brightness. "Leave me, Na-
iads!
Leave me!" he cried; "the day to me is dearer
Than all your caves deep-sphered in Ocean's quiet.
I am but mortal, seek but mortal pleasure:
I would not change this flexile, warm existence,
Though swept by storms, and shocked by Jove's dread
thunder,
To be a king beneath the dark-green waters."
Still moaned the humid lips, between their kisses,
"We have no love. O, love us, we who love thee!"
And came in answer, thus, the words of Hylas:
"My love is mortal. For the Argive maidens

I keep the kisses which your lips would ravish.
Unlock your cold white arms, — take from my shoulder
The tangled swell of your bewildering tresses.
Let me return: the wind comes down from Ida,
And soon the galley, stirring from her slumber,
Will fret to ride where Pelion's twilight shadow
Falls o'er the towers of Jason's sea-girt city.
I am not yours, — I cannot braid the lilies
In your wet hair, nor on your argent bosoms
Close my drowsed eyes to hear your rippling voices.
Hateful to me your sweet, cold, crystal being, —
Your world of watery quiet. Help, Apollo!
For I am thine: thy fire, thy beam, thy music,
Dance in my heart and flood my sense with rapture:
The joy, the warmth and passion now awaken,
Promised by thee, but erewhile calmly sleeping.
O, leave me, Naiads! loose your chill embraces,
Or I shall die, for mortal maidens pining."
But still with unrelenting arms they bound him,
And still, accordant, flowed their watery voices:
"We have thee now — we hold thy beauty prisoned;
O, come with us beneath the emerald waters!
We have no love; we love thee, rosy Hylas.
O, love us, who shall nevermore release thee:
Love us, whose milky arms will be thy cradle
Far down on the untroubled sands of ocean,

Where now we bear thee, clasped in our embraces."
And slowly, slowly sank the amorous Naiads;
The boy's blue eyes, upturned, looked through the water,
Pleading for help; but Heaven's immortal Archer
Was swathed in cloud. The ripples hid his forehead,
And last, the thick, bright curls a moment floated,
So warm and silky that the stream upbore them,
Closing reluctant, as he sank forever.

The sunset died behind the crags of Imbros.
Argo was tugging at her chain; for freshly
Blew the swift breeze, and leaped the restless billows.
The voice of Jason roused the dozing sailors,
And up the mast was heaved the snowy canvas.
But mighty Hêraclês, the Jove-begotten,
Unmindful stood, beside the cool Scamander,
Leaning upon his club. A purple chlamys
Tossed o'er an urn was all that lay before him:
And when he called, expectant, "Hylas! Hylas!"
The empty echoes made him answer—"Hylas!"

KUBLEH:

A STORY OF THE ASSYRIAN DESERT.

THE black-eyed children of the Desert drove
Their flocks together at the set of sun.
The tents were pitched; the weary camels bent
Their suppliant necks, and knelt upon the sand;
The hunters quartered by the kindled fires
The wild boars of the Tigris they had slain,
And all the stir and sound of evening ran
Throughout the Shammar camp. The dewy air
Bore its full burden of confused delight
Across the flowery plain; and while, afar,
The snows of Koordish Mountains in the ray
Flashed roseate amber, Nimroud's ancient mound
Rose broad and black against the burning West.
The shadows deepened, and the stars came out,
Sparkling in violet ether; one by one

Glimmered the ruddy camp-fires on the plain,
And shapes of steed and horseman moved among
The dusky tents, with shout and jostling cry,
And neigh and restless prancing. Children ran
To hold the thongs, while every rider drove
His quivering spear in the earth, and by his door
Tethered the horse he loved. In midst of all
Stood Shammeriyah, whom they dared not touch, —
The foal of wondrous Kubleh, to the Shekh
A dearer wealth than all his Georgian girls.

But when their meal was o'er, — when the red fires
Blazed brighter, and the dogs no longer bayed, —
When Shammar hunters with the boys sat down
To cleanse their bloody knives, came Alimàr,
The poet of the tribe, whose songs of love
Are sweeter than Bassora's nightingales, —
Whose songs of war can fire the Arab blood
Like war itself: who knows not Alimàr?
Then asked the men, "O Poet, sing of Kubleh!"
And boys laid down the burnished knives and said,
"Tell us of Kubleh, whom we never saw, —
Of wondrous Kubleh!" Closer drew the group,
With eager eyes, about the flickering fire,
While Alimàr, beneath the Assyrian stars,
Sang to the listening Arabs:

"God is great!
O Arabs! never since Mohammed rode
The sands of Beder, and by Mecca's gate
That wingèd steed bestrode, whose mane of fire
Blazed up the zenith, when, by Allah called,
He bore the Prophet to the walls of Heaven,
Was like to Kubleh, Sofuk's wondrous mare:
Not all the milk-white barbs, whose hoofs dashed
flame,
In Bagdad's stables, from the marble floor, —
Who, swathed in purple housings, pranced in state
The gay bazaars, by great Al-Raschid backed:
Not the wild charger of Mongolian breed
That went o'er half the world with Tamerlane:
Nor yet those flying coursers, long ago
From Ormuz brought by swarthy Indian grooms
To Persia's kings, — the foals of sacred mares,
Sired by the fiery stallions of the sea!

"Who ever told, in all the Desert Land,
The many deeds of Kubleh? Who can tell
Whence came she? whence her like shall come again?
O Arabs! sweet as tales of Scheherazade
Heard in the camp, when javelin shafts are tried
On the hot eve of battle, are the words
That tell the marvels of her history.

" Far in the Southern sands, the hunters say,
Did Sofuk find her, by a lonely palm.
The well had dried ; her fierce, impatient eye
Glared red and sunken, and her slight young limbs
Were lean with thirst. He checked his camel's pace,
And while it knelt, untied the water-skin,
And when the wild mare drank, she followed him.
Thence none but Sofuk might the saddle gird
Upon her back, or clasp the brazen gear
About her shining head, that brooked no curb
From even him ; for she, alike, was royal.

" Her form was lighter, in its shifting grace,
Than some impassioned almeh's, when the dance
Unbinds her scarf, and golden anklets gleam,
Through floating drapery, on the buoyant air.
Her light, free head was ever held aloft ;
Between her slender and transparent ears
The silken forelock tossed ; her nostril's arch,
Thin-blown, in proud and pliant beauty spread,
Snuffing the desert winds. Her glossy neck
Curved to the shoulder like an eagle's wing,
And all her matchless lines of flank and limb
Seemed fashioned from the flying shapes of air.
When sounds of warlike preparation rang
From tent to tent, her keen and restless eye

Shone blood-red as a ruby, and her neigh
Rang wild and sharp above the clash of spears.

"The tribes of Tigris and the Desert knew her:
Sofuk before the Shammar bands she bore
To meet the dread Jebours, who waited not
To bid her welcome; and the savage Koord,
Chased from his bold irruption on the plain,
Has seen her hoof-prints in his mountain snow.
Lithe as the dark-eyed Syrian gazelle,
O'er ledge, and chasm, and barren steep amid
The Sinjar hills, she ran the wild ass down.
Through many a battle's thickest brunt she stormed,
Reeking with sweat and dust, and fetlock deep
In curdling gore. When hot and lurid haze
Stifled the crimson sun, she swept before
The whirling sand-spout, till her gusty mane
Flared in its vortex, while the camels lay
Groaning and helpless on the fiery waste.

"The tribes of Taurus and the Caspian knew her:
The Georgian chiefs have heard her trumpet neigh
Before the walls of Teflis; pines that grow
On ancient Caucasus have harbored her,
Sleeping by Sofuk in their spicy gloom.
The surf of Trebizond has bathed her flanks,

When from the shore she saw the white-sailed bark
That brought him home from Stamboul. Never yet,
O Arabs! never yet was like to Kubleh!

"And Sofuk loved her. She was more to him
Than all his snowy-bosomed odalisques.
For many years she stood beside his tent,
The glory of the tribe.

"At last she died,—
Died, while the fire was yet in all her limbs,—
Died for the life of Sofuk, whom she loved.
The base Jebours—on whom be Allah's curse!—
Came on his path, when far from any camp,
And would have slain him, but that Kubleh sprang
Against the javelin points, and bore them down,
And gained the open Desert. Wounded sore,
She urged her light limbs into maddening speed,
And made the wind a laggard. On and on
The red sand slid beneath her, and behind
Whirled in a swift and cloudy turbulence,
As when some star of Eblis, downward hurled
By Allah's bolt, sweeps with its burning hair
The waste of darkness. On and on the bleak,
Bare ridges rose before her, came, and passed,
And every flying leap with fresher blood

Her nostril stained, till Sofuk's brow and breast
Were flecked with crimson foam. He would have
turned
To save his treasure, though himself were lost,
But Kubleh fiercely snapped the brazen rein.
At last, when through her spent and quivering frame
The sharp throes ran, our clustering tents arose,
And with a neigh, whose shrill excess of joy
O'ercame its agony, she stopped and fell.
The Shammar men came round her as she lay,
And Sofuk raised her head, and held it close
Against his breast. Her dull and glazing eye
Met his, and with a shuddering gasp she died.
Then like a child his bursting grief made way
In passionate tears, and with him all the tribe
Wept for the faithful mare.

"They dug her grave
Amid El-Hather's marbles, where she lies
Buried with ancient kings; and since that time
Was never seen, and will not be again,
O Arabs! though the world be doomed to live
As many moons as count the desert sands,
The like of glorious Kubleh. God is great!"

LOVE AND SOLITUDE.

I.

EARTH knew no deeper life since Earth began,
And scarce the Heaven above :
For us the world contains no ban ;
In the profoundest measure given to Man,
We love, we love !
O, in that sound, completion lies
For all imperfect destinies.
It is a pulse of joy, that rings
The marriage-peal of Nature, brings
The lonely heart, the humblest and the least,
To share her royal feast ;
No more an outcast on her sod,
Or at her board a stinted guest,
But now in purple raiment dressed,
And heir to all delight, that she receives of God !

II.

A balmy breath is breathed upon the land,
And through the spirit's inmost cells
It floats and swells,
Till at the touch of its persuading hand
The jealous bolts give way, and every door
Stands wide forevermore.
Not only there, dear love, not only there
Where Love's warm chambers front the morning air,
Thy soul may walk, and in the secret bower
Where burns the holiest fire that Heaven lets fall,
And with Ambition, in his blazoned hall,
Hope, in her airy tower!
The heart has other guests than these,
More secret halls, more solemn mysteries.
Dark crypts, beheld of none,
Throne darker powers, that flee the sun,
Chained far below, and heard at intervals
When all is still, and through the trembling walls
Some guilty whisper calls;
Or, when the storms have blown,
And the house rocks upon its basement stone,
They wring their chains with clamor that appals
The pale-cheeked lord. To thee

Those awful crypts and corridors are free.
Thou through the darkened hush mayst glide,
White and serene, with unaffrighted breath,
Past the blind Sins, that slumber leaden-eyed
In caves that lead to Death.
Nor I the less, where purer powers control
The perfect temple of thy soul,
And saintly harmonies to me
Breathe from its gates unceasingly,
Its bowery courts and chambers that infold
The chastened gleam of pearl and gold,
Free to the sun and blessèd air:
No deeper gloom than starry twilight there!

III.

What is the world of men to us? We love,
And Love hath his own world. Love hath
Repose in storms and peace in wrath,
Far from the shocks of Time a quiet path,
Another Earth below, another Heaven above.
Men from their weakness and their sin create
The iron bonds of State,
Soldered with wrongs of olden date,—
The heartless frame, the chance-directed law

Which grows to them a grand, avenging Fate,
And fills their darkness with its awe.
States have no soul. The World's tired brain
O'er many riddles broods with pain,
Not hopeless all, but hoping much in vain.
Those who have never loved may stay,
And in his files fight out the day;
But aliens we, who breathe a separate air
In regions far away!
Thou art my law, I thine: the links we wear,
If not of Freedom, dearer still,
And binding both in one harmonious will.
Why should we track the labyrinth of ill
Before us, — mingle with the fret
Of jangling natures, till our souls forget
Their crystal orbits of accordant sound?
Why should we walk the common ground,
Where gloom is born of gloom, and pain
From pain unfoldeth ever,
When to the blue air's limitless domain,
Made ours by right of love, we rise without endeavor?

IV.

Some voice of wind or sea
May reach the imbruted slave, and in his ear

Drop Freedom's mighty secret: so to me
Through blindness and through passion came the clear
Calm voice of Love, thenceforth to be
The revelation of diviner truth
Than ever touched our sinless youth,—
A power to bid us face Eternity!
But the same whisper that reveals the glory
Of Freedom's brow, makes also known
The bitterness of bondage. We
Will leave this splendid misery,
This hollow joy, whose laugh but hides a groan,
And teach our lives to write a perfect story.

V.

O, somewhere, in the living realms that lie
Between the icy zones of desolation,
Covered by some remote, unconscious sky,
Where God's serene creation
Yet never glassed itself in human eye,
Must be a glorious Valley, hidden
In the safe bosom of the hills that part
The river-veins of some old Continent's heart,
To love like ours a shelter unforbidden!
Some Valley must there be,
Whereto wide wastes of desert sand have kept

The gateway secret, mountain walls
Across the explorer's pathway stepped,
Or mighty woods surrounded like a sea.
Love's voice, unto the chosen ones he calls,
Alike the compass to his freedom is,
And to that Vale, the lodestar of our bliss,
Our hearts shall guide us. Even now
I see the close defiles unfold
Upon a sloping mead that lies below
A mountain black with pines,
O'er which the barren ridges heave their lines,
And high beyond, the snowy ranges old!
Fed by the plenteous mountain rain,
Southward, a blue lake sparkles, whence outflows
A rivulet's silver vein,
Awhile meandering in fair repose,
Then caught by riven cliffs that guard our home,
And flung upon the outer world in foam!
The sky above that still retreat,
Through all the year serene and sweet,
Drops dew that finds the daisy's heart,
And keeps the violet's tender lids apart:
All winds that whistle drearily
Around the naked granite, die
With many a long, melodious sigh
Among the pines; and if a tempest seek

The summits cold and bleak,
He does but shift the snow from shining peak to peak.

VI.

Or should this Valley seem
Too deeply buried from the golden sun,
Still may a home be won
Whose breast lies open to his every beam.
Some Island, on the purple plain
Of Polynesian main,
Where never yet the adventurer's prore
Lay rocking near its coral shore:
A tropic mystery, which the enamoured Deep
Folds, as a beauty in a charmèd sleep.
There lofty palms, of some imperial line,
That never bled their nimble wine,
Crowd all the hills, and out the headlands go
To watch on distant reefs the lazy brine
Turning its fringe of snow.
There, when the sun stands high
Upon the burning summit of the sky,
All shadows wither: Light alone
Is in the world: and, pregnant grown
With teeming life, the trembling island-earth

And panting sea forebode sweet pains of birth
Which never come, — their love brings never forth
The Human Soul they lack alone!

VII.

We to that Island soul and voice will be,
When (rapturous hour!) the baffling quest is over,
The boat is wrecked, the ship is blown to sea,
And underneath the palm-tree's cover
We bless our God that He hath left us free.
Then, wandering through the inland dells
Where sun and dew have built their gorgeous bowers,
The golden, blue, and crimson flowers
Will drain in joy their spicy wells,
The lily toll her alabaster bells,
And some fine influence, unknown and sweet,
Precede our happy feet
Around the Isle, till all the life that dwells
In leaf and stem shall feel it, and awake,
And even the pearly-bosomed shells,
Wet with the foamy kiss of lingering swells,
Shall rosier beauty at our coming take,
For Love's dear sake!
There when, like Aphrodite, Morn
From the ecstatic waves is born,

The chieftain Palm, that tops each mountain-crest,
Shall feel her glory gild his scaly greaves,
And lift his glittering leaves
Like arms outspread, to take her to his breast.
Then shall we watch her slowly bend, and fold
The Island in her arms of gold,
Breathing away the heavy balms which crept
All night around the bowers, and lifting up
Each flower's enamelled cup,
To drink the sweetness gathered while it slept.
Yet on our souls a joy more tender
Shall gently sink, when sunset makes the sky
One burning sheet of opalescent splendor,
And on the deep dissolving rainbows lie.
No whisper shall disturb
That alchemy superb,
Whereto our beings every sense surrender.
O, long and sweet, while sitting side by side,
Looking across the western sea,
That dream of Death, that morn of Heaven, shall be;
And when the shadows hide
Each dying flush, upon the quiet tide,—
Quiet as is our love,—
We first shall see the stars come out above,
And after them, the slanting beams that run,
Based on the sea, far up the shining track

Of the emblazoned Zodiac,
A pyramid of light, above the buried sun!

VIII.

There shall our lives to such accordance grow
As love alone can know;
Can never know but there:
Each within each involved, like Light and Air,
In endless marriage. Earth will fill
Her bounteous lap with all we ask of Earth,
Nor ever drought or dearth
Shrink the rich pulps of vale and hill.
Content at last the missing tone to hear
Through all her summer-chords,
Which makes their full-strung harmony complete
In her delighted ear,
She to our hearts that concord shall repeat.
Led by the strain, it may be ours to enter
The secret chamber where she works alone
With Color, Form, and Tone,
In human mood, or, sterner grown,
Takes hold on powers that shake her fiery centre.
Year after year the Island shall become
A fairer and serener home,

And happy children, beautiful as Dawn,
The future parents of a race
Whose purer eyes shall face to face
Look on the Angels, fill our place,
And be the Presence and the Soul, when we have gone.

IX.

Forgive the dream. Love owns no human birth,
And may not find fulfilment here
On this degenerate Earth.
Forgive the dream : here never yet was given
More than the promise and the hope of Heaven.
The dearest joy is dashed with fear,
Our darkest sorrow may be then most near.
Even with the will our passion lends
We cannot break the chain ;
Against our vows, we must remain
With common men, and compass common ends.
We cannot shut our hearts from haunting fears ;
We cannot purge our eyes from heavy tears ;
We cannot shift the burden and the woe
Which all alike must know,
Which Love's Elected through the countless years
Have known, and, knowing, died : God wills it so.

MON-DA-MIN;

OR, THE ROMANCE OF MAIZE.

I.

LONG ere the shores of green America
Were touched by men of Norse and Saxon blood,
What time the Continent in silence lay,
A solemn world of forest and of flood,
Where Nature wantoned wild in zones immense,
Unconscious of her own magnificence;

II.

Then to the savage race, who knew no world
Beyond the hunter's lodge, the council-fire,
The clouds of grosser sense were sometimes furled,
And spirits came to answer their desire,—
The spirits of the race, grotesque and shy;
Exaggerated powers of earth and sky.

III.

For Gods resemble whom they govern: they,
The fathers of the soil, may not outgrow
The children's vision. In that earlier day,
They stooped the race familiarly to know;
From Heaven's blue prairies they descended then,
And took the shapes and shared the lives of men.

IV.

A chief there was, who in the frequent stress
Of want, yet in contentment, lived his days;
His lodge was built within the wilderness
Of Huron, clasping those transparent bays,
Those deeps of unimagined crystal, where
The bark canoe seems hung in middle air.

V.

There, from the lake and from the uncertain chase,
With patient heart his sustenance he drew;
And he was glad to see, in that wild place,
The sons and daughters that around him grew,
Although more scant they made his scanty store,
And in the winter moons his need was sore.

VI.

The eldest was a boy, a silent lad,
Who wore a look of wisdom from his birth;
Such beauty, both of form and face, he had,
As until then was never known on earth:
And so he was (his soul so bright and far!)
Osséo named, — Son of the Evening Star.

VII.

This boy by nature was companionless:
His soul drew nurture only when it sucked
The savage dugs of Fable; he could guess
The knowledge other minds but slowly plucked
From out the heart of things; to him, as well
As to his Gods, all things were possible.

VIII.

The heroes of that shapeless faith of his
Took life from him: when gusts of powdery snow
Whirled round the lodge, he saw Paup-puckewiss
Floundering amid the drifts, and he would go
Climbing the hills, while sunset faded wan,
To seek the feathers of the Rosy Swan.

IX.

He knew the lord of serpent and of beast,
The crafty Incarnation of the North;
He knew, when airs grew warm and buds increased,
The sky was pierced, the Summer issued forth,
And when a cloud concealed some mountain's crest,
The Bird of Thunder brooded on his nest.

X.

Through Huron's mists he saw the enchanted boat
Of old Mishosha to his island go,
And oft he watched, if on the waves might float,
As once, the Fiery Plume of Wassamo;
And when the moonrise flooded coast and bay,
He climbed the headland, stretching far away;

XI.

For there — so ran the legend — nightly came
The small Puck-wudjees, ignorant of harm:
The friends of Man, in many a sportive game
The nimble elves consoled them for the charm
Which kept them exiled from their homes afar, —
The silver lodges of a twilight star.

XII.

So grew Osséo, as a lonely pine,
That knows the secret of the wandering breeze,
And ever sings its canticles divine,
Uncomprehended by the other trees:
And now the time drew nigh, when he began
The solemn fast whose issue proves the man.

XIII.

His father built a lodge the wood within,
Where he the appointed space should duly bide,
Till such propitious time as he had been
By faith prepared, by fasting purified,
And in mysterious dreams allowed to see
What God the guardian of his life would be.

XIV.

The anxious crisis of the Spring was past,
And warmth was master o'er the lingering cold.
The alder's catkins dropped; the maple cast
His crimson bloom, the willow's downy gold
Blew wide, and softer than a squirrel's ear
The white-oak's foxy leaves began appear.

XV.

There was a motion in the soil. A sound
Lighter than falling seeds, shook out of flowers,
Exhaled where dead leaves, sodden on the ground,
Repressed the eager grass; and there for hours
Osséo lay, and vainly strove to bring
Into his mind the miracle of Spring.

XVI.

The wood-birds knew it, and their voices rang
Around his lodge; with many a dart and whir
Of saucy joy, the shrewish catbird sang
Full-throated, and he heard the kingfisher,
Who from his God escaped with rumpled crest,
And the white medal hanging on his breast.

XVII.

The aquilegia sprinkled on the rocks
A scarlet rain; the yellow violet
Sat in the chariot of its leaves; the phlox
Held spikes of purple flame in meadows wet,
And all the streams with vernal-scented reed
Were fringed, and streaky bells of miskodeed.

XVIII.

The boy went musing: What are these, that burst
The sod and grow, without the aid of man?
What father brought them food? what mother nursed
Them in her earthy lodge, till Spring began?
They cannot speak; they move but with the air;
Yet souls of evil or of good they bear.

XIX.

How are they made, that some with wholesome juice
Delight the tongue, and some are charged with death?
If spirits them inhabit, they can loose
Their shape sometimes, and talk with human breath:
Would that in dreams one such would come to me,
And thence my teacher and my guardian be!

XX.

So, when more languid with his fast, the boy
Kept to his lodge, he pondered much thereon,
And other memories gave his mind employ;
Memories of winters when the moose were gone,—
When tales of Manabozo failed to melt
The hunger-pang his pining brothers felt.

XXI.

He thought: The Mighty Spirit knows all things,
Is master over all. Could He not choose
Design his children food to ease the stings
Of hunger, when the lake and wood refuse?
If He will bless me with the knowledge, I
Will for my brothers fast until I die.

XXII.

Four days were sped since he had tasted meat;
Too faint he was to wander any more,
When from the open sky, that, blue and sweet,
Looked in upon him through the lodge's door,
With quiet gladness he beheld a fair
Celestial Shape descending through the air.

XXIII.

He fell serenely, as a wingèd seed
Detached in summer from the maple bough;
His glittering clothes unruffled by the speed,
The tufted plumes unshaken on his brow:
Bright, wonderful, he came without a sound,
And like a burst of sunshine struck the ground.

XXIV.

So light he stood, so tall and straight of limb,
So fair the heavenly freshness of his face,
With beating heart Osséo looked at him,
For now a God had visited the place.
More brave a God his dreams had never seen:
The stranger's garments were a shining green,

XXV.

Sheathing his limbs in many a stately fold,
That, parting on his breast, allowed the eye
To note beneath, his vest of scaly gold,
Whereon the drops of slaughter, scarcely dry,
Disclosed their blushing stain: his shoulders fair
Gave to the wind long tufts of silky hair.

XXVI.

The plumy crest, that high and beautiful
Above his head its branching tassels hung,
Shook down a golden dust, while, fixing full
His eyes upon the boy, he loosed his tongue.
Deep in his soul Osséo did rejoice
To hear the reedy music of his voice:

XXVII.

"By the Great Spirit I am hither sent
He knows the wishes whereupon you feed,—
The soul, that, on your brothers' good intent,
Would sink ambition to relieve their need:
This thing is grateful to the Master's eye,
Nor will His wisdom what you seek deny.

XXVIII.

"But blessings are not free; they do not fall
In listless hands; by toil the soul must prove
Its steadfast purpose master over all,
Before their wings in pomp of coming move:
Here, wrestling with me, must you overcome,
In me, the secret,—else, my lips are dumb."

XXIX.

No match for his, Osséo's limbs appeared,
Weak with the fast; and yet in soul he grew
Composed and resolute, by accents cheered,
That spake in light what he but darkly knew.
He rose, unto the issue nerved; he sent
Into his arms the hope of the event.

XXX.

The shining stranger wrestled long and hard,
When, disengaging weary limbs, he said:
" It is enough ; with no unkind regard
The Master's eye your toil hath visited.
He bids me cease ; to-day let strife remain ;
But on the morrow I will come again."

XXXI.

And on the morrow came he as before,
Dropping serenely down the deep-blue air:
More weak and languid was the boy, yet more
Courageous he, that crowning test to bear.
His soul so wrought in every fainting limb,
It seemed the cruel fast had strengthened him.

XXXII.

Again they grappled, and their sinews wrung
In desperate emulation; and again
Came words of comfort from the stranger's tongue
When they had ceased. He scaled the heavenly plain,
His tall, bright stature lessening as he rose,
Till lost amid the infinite repose.

XXXIII.

On the third day descending as before,
His raiment's gleam surprised the silent sky;
And weaker still the poor boy felt, yet more
Courageous he, and resolute to die,
So he might first the promised good embrace,
And leave a blessing unto all his race.

XXXIV.

This time with intertwining limbs they strove;
The God's green mantle shook in every fold,
And o'er Osséo's heated forehead drove
His silky hair, his tassel's dusty gold,
Till, spent and breathless, he at last forbore,
And sat to rest beside the lodge's door.

XXXV.

"My friend," he said, "the issue now is plain;
Who wrestles in his soul must victor be;
Who bids his life in payment shall attain
The end he seeks — and you will vanquish me.
Then, these commands fulfilling, you shall win
What the Great Spirit gives in Mon-da-Min.

XXXVI.

" When I am dead, strip off this green array,
And pluck the tassels from my shrivelled hair;
Then bury me where summer rains shall play
Above my breast, and sunshine linger there.
Remove the matted sod; for I would have
The earth lie lightly, softly on my grave.

XXXVII.

" And tend the place, lest any noxious weed
Through the sweet soil should strike its bitter root;
Nor let the blossoms of the forest breed,
Nor the wild grass in green luxuriance shoot;
But when the earth is dry and blistered, fold
Thereon the fresh and dainty-smelling mould.

XXXVIII.

" The clamoring crow, the blackbird swarms that make
The meadow trees their hive, must come not near;
Scare thence all hurtful things; nor quite forsake
Your careful watch until the woods appear
With crimson blotches deeply dashed and crossed,—
Sign of the fatal pestilence of Frost.

XXXIX.

"This done, the secret, into knowledge grown,
Is yours forevermore." With that, he took
The yielding air. Osséo, left alone,
Followed his flight with hope-enraptured look.
The pains of hunger fled; a happy flame
Danced in his heart until the trial came.

XL.

It happened so, as Mon-da-Min foretold:
Osséo's soul, at every wreathing twist
Of palpitating muscle, grew more bold,
And from the limbs of his antagonist
Celestial vigor to his own he drew,
Till with one mighty heave he overthrew.

XLI.

Then from the body, beautiful and cold,
He stripped the shining clothes; but on his breast
He left the vest, engrained with blushing gold,
And covered him in decent burial-rest.
At sunset to his father's lodge he passed,
And soothed with meat the anguish of his fast.

XLII.

Nought did he speak of all that he had done,
But day by day in secrecy he sought
An opening in the forest, where the sun
Warmed the new grave: so tenderly he wrought,
So lightly heaped the mould, so carefully
Kept all the place from choking herbage free,

XLIII.

That in a little while a folded plume
Pushed timidly the covering soil aside,
And, fed by fattening rains, took broader room,
Until it grew a stalk, and rustled wide
Its leafy garments, lifting in the air
Its tasselled top, and knots of silky hair.

XLIV.

Osséo marvelled to behold his friend
In this fair plant; the secret of the Spring
Was his at length; and till the Summer's end
He guarded him from every harmful thing.
He scared the cloud of blackbirds, wheeling low;
His arrow pierced the reconnoitring crow.

XLV.

Now came the brilliant mornings, kindling all
The woody hills with pinnacles of fire ;
The gum's ensanguined leaves began to fall,
The buckeye blazed in prodigal attire,
And frosty vapors left the lake at night
To string the prairie grass with spangles white.

XLVI.

One day, from long and unsuccessful chase
The chief returned. Osséo through the wood
In silence led him to the guarded place,
Where now the plant in golden ripeness stood.
" Behold, my father ! " he exclaimed, " our friend,
Whom the Great Spirit unto me did send.

XLVII.

" Then, when I fastèd, and my prayer He knew,
That He would save my brothers from their want ;
For this, His messenger I overthrew,
And from his grave was born this glorious plant.
'Tis Mon-da-Min : his sheathing husks enclose
Food for my brothers in the time of snows.

XLVIII.

"I leave you now, my father! Here befits
Me longer not to dwell. My pathway lies
To where the West Wind on the mountain sits,
And the Red Swan beyond the sunset flies:
There may superior wisdom be in store."
And so he went, and he returned no more.

XLIX.

But Mon-da-Min remained, and still remains;
His children cover all the boundless land,
And the warm sun and frequent mellow rains
Shape the tall stalks and make the leaves expand.
A mighty army they have grown: he drills
Their green battalions on the summer hills.

L.

And when the silky hair hangs crisp and dead,
Then leave their rustling ranks the tasselled peers,
In broad encampment pitch their tents instead,
And garner up the ripe autumnal ears:
The annual storehouse of a nation's need,
From whose abundance all the world may feed.

THE SOLDIER AND THE PARD.

A SECOND deluge! Well, — no matter: here,
At least, is better shelter than the lean,
Sharp-elbowed oaks — a dismal company!
That stood around us in the mountain road
When that cursed axle broke: a roof of thatch,
A fire of withered boughs, and best of all,
This ruddy wine of Languedoc, that warms
One through and through, from heart to finger-ends.
No better quarters for a stormy night
A soldier, like myself, could ask; and since
The rough Cevennes refuse to let us forth,
Why, fellow-travellers, if so you will,
I'll tell the story cut so rudely short
When both fore-wheels broke from the diligence,
Stocked in the rut, and pitched us all together:

I said, we fought beside the Pyramids ;
And somehow, from the glow of this good wine,
And from the gloomy rain, that shuts one in
With his own self, — a sorry mate sometimes ! —
The scene comes back like life. As then, I feel
The sun, and breathe the hot Egyptian air,
Hear Kleber, see the sabre of Dessaix
Flash at the column's front, and in the midst
Napoleon, upon his Barbary horse,
Calm, swarthy-browed, and wiser than the Sphinx
Whose granite lips guard Egypt's mystery.
Ha ! what a rout ! our cannon bellowed round
The Pyramids : the Mamelukes closed in,
And hand to hand like devils did we fight,
Rolled towards Sakkara in the smoke and sand.

For days we followed up the Nile. We pitched
Our tents in Memphis, pitched them on the site
Of Antinoë, and beside the cliffs
Of Aboufayda. Then we came anon
On Kenneh, ere the sorely-frightened Bey
Had time to pack his harem : nay, we took
His camels, not his wives : and so, from day
To day, past wrecks of temples half submerged
In sandy inundation, till we saw
Old noseless Memnon sitting on the plain,

Both hands upon his knees, and in the east
Karnak's propylon and its pillared court.
The sphinxes wondered — such as had a face —
To see us stumbling down their avenues;
But we kept silent. One may whistle round
Your Roman temples here at Nismes, or dance
Upon the Pont du Gard; — but, take my word,
Egyptian ruins are a serious thing:
You would not dare let fly a joke beside
The maimed colossi, though your very feet
Might catch between some mummied Pharaoh's ribs.

Dessaix was bent on chasing Mamelukes,
And so we rummaged tomb and catacomb,
Clambered the hills and watched the Desert's rim
For sight of horse. One day my company
(I was but ensign then) found far within
The sands, a two-days' journey from the Nile,
A round oasis, like a jewel set.
It was a grove of date-trees, clustering close
About a tiny spring, whose overflow
Trickled beyond their shade a little space,
And the insatiate Desert licked it up.
The fiery ride, the glare of afternoon
Had burned our faces, so we stopped to feel
The coolness and the shadow, like a bath

Of pure ambrosial lymph, receive our limbs
And sweeten every sense. Drowsed by the soft,
Delicious greenness and repose, I crept
Into a balmy nest of yielding shrubs,
And floated off to slumber on a cloud
Of rapturous sensation.

When I woke,
So deep had been the oblivion of that sleep,
That Adam, when he woke in Paradise,
Was not more blank of knowledge; he had felt
As heedlessly, the silence and the shade;
As ignorantly had raised his eyes and seen —
As, for a moment, I — what then I saw
With terror, freezing limb and voice like death,
When the slow sense, supplying one lost link,
Ran with electric fleetness through the chain
And showed me what I was, — no miracle,
But lost and left alone amid the waste,
Fronting a deadly Pard, that kept great eyes
Fixed steadily on mine. I could not move:
My heart beat slow and hard: I sat and gazed,
Without a wink, upon those jasper orbs,
Noting the while, with horrible detail
Whereto my fascinated sight was bound,
Their tawny brilliance, and the spotted fell

That wrinkled round them, smoothly sloping back
And curving to the short and tufted ears.
I felt — and with a sort of fearful joy —
The beauty of the creature : 'twas a pard,
Not such as one of those they show you caged
In Paris, — lean and scurvy beasts enough !
No : but a desert pard, superb and proud,
That would have died behind the cruel bars.

I think the creature had not looked on man,
For, as my brain grew cooler, I could see
Small sign of fierceness in her eyes, but chief,
Surprise and wonder. More and more entranced,
Her savage beauty warmed away the chill
Of deathlike terror at my heart : I stared
With kindling admiration, and there came
A gradual softness o'er the flinty light
Within her eyes ; a shadow crept around
Their yellow disks, and something like a dawn
Of recognition of superior will,
Of brute affection, sympathy enslaved
By higher nature, then informed her face.
Thrilling in every nerve, I stretched my hand, —
She silent, moveless, — touched her velvet head,
And with a warm, sweet shiver in my blood,
Stroked down the ruffled hairs. She did not start ;

But, in a moment's lapse, drew up one paw
And moved a step, — another, — till her breath
Came hot upon my face. She stopped: she rolled
A deep-voiced note of pleasure and of love,
And gathering up her spotted length, lay down,
Her head upon my lap, and forward thrust
One heavy-moulded paw across my knees,
The glittering talons sheathing tenderly.
Thus we, in that oasis all alone,
Sat when the sun went down: the Pard and I,
Caressing and caressed: and more of love
And more of confidence between us came,
I grateful for my safety, she alive
With the dumb pleasure of companionship,
Which touched with instincts of humanity
Her brutish nature. When I slept, at last,
My arm was on her neck.

The morrow brought
No rupture of the bond between us twain.
The creature loved me; she would bounding come,
Cat-like, to rub her great, smooth, yellow head
Against my knee, or with rough tongue would lick
The hand that stroked the velvet of her hide.
How beautiful she was! how lithe and free
The undulating motions of her frame!

How shone, like isles of tawny gold, her spots,
Mapped on the creamy white! And when she walked,
No princess, with the crown about her brows,
Looked so superbly royal. Ah, my friends,
Smile as you may, but I would give this life
With its fantastic pleasures — ay, even that
One leads in Paris — to be back again
In the red Desert with my splendid Pard.

That grove of date-trees was our home, our world,
A star of verdure in a sky of sand.
Without the feathery fringes of its shade
The naked Desert ran, its burning round
Sharp as a sword: the naked sky above,
Awful in its immensity, not shone
There only, where the sun supremely flamed,
But all its deep-blue walls were penetrant
With dazzling light. God reigned in Heaven and Earth,
An Everlasting Presence, and his care
Fed us, alike his children. From the trees
That shook down pulpy dates, and from the spring,
The quiet author of that happy grove,
My wants were sated; and when midnight came,
Then would the Pard steal softly from my side,
Take the unmeasured sand with flying leaps

And vanish in the dusk, returning soon
With a gazelle's light carcass in her jaws.
So passed the days, and each the other taught
Our simple language. She would come at call
Of the pet name I gave her, bound and sport
When so I bade, and she could read my face
Through all its changing moods, with better skill
Than many a Christian comrade. Pard and beast,
Though you may say she was, she had a soul.

But Sin will find the way to Paradise.
Ere long the sense of isolation fed
My mind with restless fancies. I began
To miss the life of camp, the march, the fight,
The soldier's emulation: youthful blood
Ran in my veins: the silence lost its charm,
And when the morning sunrise lighted up
The threshold of the Desert, I would gaze
With looks of bitter longing o'er the sand.
At last, I filled my soldier's sash with dates,
Drank deeply of the spring, and while the Pard
Roamed in the starlight for her forage, took
A westward course. The grove already lay
A dusky speck — no more — when through the night
Came the forsaken creature's eager cry.
Into a sandy pit I crept, and heard

Her bounding on my track until she rolled
Down from the brink upon me. Then with cries
Of joy and of distress, the touching proof
Of the poor beast's affection, did she strive
To lift me — Pardon, friends! these foolish eyes
Must have their will: and had you seen her then,
In her mad gambols, as we homeward went,
Your hearts had softened too.

But I, possessed
By some vile devil of mistrust, became
More jealous and impatient. In my heart
I cursed the grove, and with suspicions wronged
The noble Pard. She keeps me here, I thought,
Deceived with false caresses, as a cat
Toys with the trembling mouse she straight devours.
Will she so gently fawn about my feet,
When the gazelles are gone? Will she crunch dates,
And drink the spring, whose only drink is blood?
Am I to ruin flattered, and by whom? —
Not even a man, a wily beast of prey.
Thus did the Devil whisper in mine ear,
Till those black thoughts were rooted in my heart
And made me cruel. So it chanced one day,
That as I watched a flock of birds, that wheeled,
And dipped, and circled in the air, the Pard,

Moved by a freak of fond solicitude
To win my notice, closed her careful fangs
About my knee. Scarce knowing what I did,
In the blind impulse of suspicious fear,
I plunged, full home, my dagger in her neck.
God! could I but recall that blow! She loosed
Her hold, as softly as a lover quits
His mistress' lips, and with a single groan,
Full of reproach and sorrow, sank and died.
What had I done! Sure never on this earth
Did sharper grief so base a deed requite.
Its murderous fury gone, my heart was racked
With pangs of wild contrition, spent itself
In cries and tears, the while I called on God
To curse me for my sin. There lay the Pard,
Her splendid eyes all film, her blazoned fell
Smirched with her blood; and I, her murderer,
Less than a beast, had thus repaid her love.

Ah, friends! with all this guilty memory
My heart is sore: and little now remains
To tell you, but that afterwards — how long,
I could not know — our soldiers picked me up,
Wandering about the Desert, wild with grief
And sobbing like a child. My nerves have grown
To steel, in many battles; I can step

Without a shudder through the heaps of slain;
But never, never, till the day I die,
Prevent a woman's weakness when I think
Upon my desert Pard: and if a man
Deny this truth she taught me, to his face
I say he lies: a beast may have a soul.

ARIEL IN THE CLOVEN PINE.

Now the frosty stars are gone :
I have watched them, one by one,
Fading on the shores of Dawn.
Round and full the glorious sun
Walks with level step the spray,
Through his vestibule of Day,
While the wolves that late did howl
Slink to dens and coverts foul,
Guarded by the demon owl,
Who, last night, with mocking croon,
Wheeled athwart the chilly moon,
And with eyes that blankly glared
On my direful torment stared.

The lark is flickering in the light ;
Still the nightingale doth sing ; —
All the isle, alive with Spring,
Lies, a jewel of delight,

On the blue sea's heaving breast:
Not a breath from out the West,
But some balmy smell doth bring
From the sprouting myrtle buds,
Or from meadowy vales that lie
Like a green inverted sky,
Which the yellow cowslip stars,
And the bloomy almond woods,
Cloud-like, cross with roseate bars.
All is life that I can spy,
To the farthest sea and sky,
And my own the only pain
Within this ring of Tyrrhene main.

In the gnarled and cloven Pine
Where that hell-born hag did chain me,
All this orb of cloudless shine,
All this youth in Nature's veins
Tingling with the season's wine,
With a sharper torment pain me.
Pansies in soft April rains
Fill their stalks with honeyed sap
Drawn from Earth's prolific lap;
But the sluggish blood she brings
To the tough Pine's hundred rings,
Closer locks their cruel hold,

Closer draws the scaly bark
Round the crevice, damp and cold,
Where my useless wings I fold,—
Sealing me in iron dark.
By this coarse and alien state
Is my dainty essence wronged;
Finer senses that belonged
To my freedom, chafe at Fate,
Till the happier elves I hate,
Who in moonlight dances turn
Underneath the palmy fern,
Or in light and twinkling bands
Follow on with linkèd hands
To the Ocean's yellow sands.

Primrose-eyes each morning ope
In their cool, deep beds of grass;
Violets make the airs that pass
Telltales of their fragrant slope.
I can see them where they spring
Never brushed by fairy wing.
All those corners I can spy
In the island's solitude,
Where the dew is never dry,
Nor the miser bees intrude.

Cups of rarest hue are there,
Full of perfumed wine undrained,—
Mushroom banquets, ne'er profaned,
Canopied by maiden-hair.
Pearls I see upon the sands,
Never touched by other hands,
And the rainbow bubbles shine
On the ridged and frothy brine,
Tenantless of voyager
Till they burst in vacant air.
O, the songs that sung might be,
And the mazy dances woven,
Had that witch ne'er crossed the sea
And the Pine been never cloven!

Many years my direst pain
Has made the wave-rocked isle complain.
Winds, that from the Cyclades
Came, to blow in wanton riot
Round its shore's enchanted quiet,
Bore my wailings on the seas;
Sorrowing birds in Autumn went
Through the world with my lament.
Still the bitter fate is mine,
All delight unshared to see,

Smarting in the cloven Pine,
While I wait the tardy axe
Which, perchance, shall set me free
From the damned witch, Sycorax.

THE HARP: AN ODE.

I.

When bleak winds through the Northern pines were
sweeping,
Some hero-skald, reclining on the sand,
Attuned it first, the chords harmonious keeping
With murmuring forest and with moaning strand:
And when, at night, the horns of mead foamed over,
And torches flared around the wassail board,
It breathed no song of maid, nor sigh of lover,
It rang aloud the triumphs of the sword!
It mocked the thunders of the ice-ribbed ocean,
With clenched hands beating back the dragon's
prow;
It gave Berserker arms their battle motion,
And swelled the red veins on the Viking's brow!

II.

No myrtle, plucked in dalliance, ever sheathed it,
  To melt the savage ardor of its flow;
The only gauds wherewith its lord enwreathed it,
  The lusty fir and Druid mistletoe.
Thus bound, it kept the old, accustomed cadence,
  Whether it pealed through slumberous ilex bowers
In stormy wooing of Byzantine maidens,
  Or shook Trinacria's languid lap of flowers;
Whether Genseric's conquering march it chanted,
  Till cloudy Atlas rang with Gothic staves,
Or where gray Calpè's pillared feet are planted,
  Died grandly out upon the unknown waves!

III.

Not unto Scania's bards alone belonging,
  The craft that loosed its tongues of changing sound,
For Ossian played, and ghosts of heroes, thronging,
  Leaned on their spears above the misty mound.
The Cambrian eagle, round his eyrie winging,
  Heard the wild chant through mountain-passes rolled,
When bearded throats chimed in with mighty singing,
  And monarchs listened, in their torques of gold:

Its dreary wail, blent with the sea-mews' clangor,
  Surged round the lonely keep of Penmaen-Mawr;
It pealed aloud, in battle's glorious anger,
  Behind the banner of the Blazing Star!

IV.

The strings are silent; who shall dare to wake them,
  Though later deeds demand their living powers?
Silent in other lands, what hand shall make them
  Leap as of old, to shape the songs of ours?
Here, while the sapless bulk of Europe moulders,
  Springs the rich blood to hero-veins unsealed,—
Source of that Will, that on its fearless shoulders
  Would bear the world's fate lightly as a shield:
Here moves a larger life, to grander measures
  Beneath our sky and through our forests rung;
Why sleeps the harp, forgetful of its treasures,—
  Buried in songs that never yet were sung?

V.

Great, solemn songs, that with majestic sounding
  Should swell the Nation's heart from sea to sea;
Informed with power, with earnest hope abounding,
  And prophecies of triumph yet to be!

Songs, by the wild wind for a thousand ages
  Hummed o'er our central prairies, vast and lone ;
Glassed by the Northern lakes in crystal pages,
  And carved by hills on pinnacles of stone ;
Songs chanted now, where undiscovered fountains
  Make in the wilderness their babbling home,
And through the deep-hewn cañons of the mountains
  Plunge the cold rivers in perpetual foam !

VI.

Sung but by these : our forests have no voices ;
  Rapt with no loftier strain our rivers roll ;
Far in the sky, no song-crowned peak rejoices
  In words that give the silent air a soul.
Wake, mighty Harp ! and thrill the shores that hearken
  For the first peal of thine immortal rhyme :
Call from the shadows that begin to darken
  The beaming forms of our heroic time :
Sing us of deeds, that on thy strings outsoaring
  The ancient soul they glorified so long,
Shall win the world to hear thy grand restoring,
  And own thy latest thy sublimest song !

SERAPION.

Come hither, Child! thou silent, shy
Young creature of the glorious eye!
Though never yet by ruder air
Than father's kiss or mother's prayer
Were stirred the tendrils of thy hair,
The sadness of a soul that stands
Withdrawn from Childhood's frolic bands,
A stranger in the land, I trace
Upon thy brow's cherubic grace
The tender pleading of thy face,
Where other stars than Joy and Hope
Have cast thy being's horoscope.

For thee, the threshold of the world
Is yet with morning dews impearled;
The nameless radiance of Birth
Imbathes thy atmosphere of Earth,

And, like a finer sunshine, swims
Round every motion of thy limbs:
The sweet, sad wonder and surprise
Of waking glimmers in thine eyes,
And wiser instinct, purer sense,
And gleams of rare intelligence
Betray the converse held by thee
In the angelic family.

Come hither, Boy! For while I press
Thy lips' confiding tenderness,
Less broad and dark the spaces be
Which Life has set 'twixt thee and me.
Thy soul's white feet shall soon depart
On paths I walked with eager heart;
God give thee, in His kindly grace,
A brighter road, a loftier place!
I see thy generous nature flow
In boundless trust to friend and foe,
And leap, despite of shocks and harms,
To clasp the world in loving arms.
I see that glorious circle shrink
Back to thy feet, at Manhood's brink,
Narrowed to one, one image fair,
And all its splendor gathered there.

The shackles of experience then
Sit lightly as on meaner men:
In flinty paths thy feet may bleed,
Thorns pierce thy flesh, thou shalt not heed,
Till when, all panting from the task,
Thine arms outspread their right shall ask,
Thine arms outspread that right shall fly,
The star shall burst, the splendor die!
Go, with thy happier brothers play,
As heedless and as wild as they;
Seek not so soon thy separate way,
Thou lamb in Childhood's field astray!

Whence camest thou? what angel bore
Thee past so many a fairer shore
Of guarding love, and guidance mild,
To drop thee on this barren wild?
Thy soul is lonely as a star,
When all its fellows muffled are,—
A single star, whose light appears
To glimmer through subduing tears.
The father who begat thee sees
In thee no deeper mysteries
Than load his heavy ledger's page,
And swell for him thy heritage.

A hard, cold man, of punctual face,
Renowned in Credit's holy-place,
Whose very wrinkles seem arrayed
In cunning hieroglyphs of trade, —
Whose gravest thought but just unlocks
The problems of uncertain stocks, —
Whose farthest flights of hope extend
From dividend to dividend.
Thy mother, — but a mother's name
Too sacred is, too sweet for blame.
No doubt she loves thee, — loves the shy,
Strange beauty of thy glorious eye;
Loves the soft mouth, whose drooping line
Is silent music; loves to twine
Thy silky hair in ringlets trim;
To watch thy lightsome play of limb;
But, God forgive me! I, who find
The soul within that beauty shrined,
I love thee more, I know thy worth
Better, than she who gave thee birth.

Are they thy keepers? They would thrust
The priceless jewel in the dust;
Would tarnish in their careless hold
The vessel of celestial gold.

Who gave them thee? What fortune lent
Their hands the delicate instrument,
Which finer hands might teach to hymn
The harmonies of Seraphim,
Which they shall make discordant soon,
The sweet bells jangled, out of tune?
Mine eyes are dim: I cannot see
The purposes of Destiny,
But than my love Heaven could not shine
More lovingly, if thou wert mine!
Rest then securely on my heart:
Give me thy trust: *my* child thou art,
And I shall lead thee through the years
To Hopes and Passions, Loves and Fears,
Till, following up Life's endless plan,
A strong and self-dependent Man,
I see thee stand and strive with men:
Thy Father now, thy Brother then.

Moan, ye wild winds! around the pane,
And fall, thou drear December rain!
Fill with your gusts the sullen day,
Tear the last clinging leaves away!
Reckless as yonder naked tree,
No blast of yours can trouble me.

Give me your chill and wild embrace,
And pour your baptism on my face;
Sound in mine ears the airy moan
That sweeps in desolate monotone,
Where on the unsheltered hill-top beat
The marches of your homeless feet!

Moan on, ye winds! and pour, thou rain!
Your stormy sobs and tears are vain,

If shed for her whose fading eyes
Will open soon on Paradise :
The eye of Heaven shall blinded be,
Or ere ye cease, if shed for me.

TAURUS.

I.

THE Scorpion's stars crawl down behind the sun,
And when he drops below the verge of day,
The glittering fangs, their fervid courses run,
Cling to his skirts and follow him away.
Then, ere the heels of flying Capricorn
Have touched the western mountain's fading rim,
I mark, stern Taurus, through the twilight gray
The glinting of thy horn,
And sullen front, uprising large and dim,
Bent to the starry hunter's sword, at bay.

II.

Thy hoofs, unwilling, climb the sphery vault;
Thy red eye trembles with an angry glare,
When the hounds follow, and in fierce assault
Bay through the fringes of the lion's hair.
The stars that once were mortal in their love,
And by their love are made immortal now,
Cluster like golden bees upon thy mane,
When thou, possessed with Jove,
Bore sweet Europa's garlands on thy brow
And stole her from the green Sicilian plain.

III.

Type of the stubborn force that will not bend
To loftier art, — soul of defiant breath
That blindly stands and battles to the end,
Nerving resistance with the throes of death, —
Majestic Taurus! when thy wrathful eye
Flamed brightest, and thy hoofs a moment stay
Their march at Night's meridian, I was born:
But in the western sky,
Like sweet Europa, Love's fair star delayed,
To hang her garland on thy silver horn.

IV.

Thou giv'st that temper of enduring mould,
That slights the wayward bent of Destiny, —
Such as sent forth the shaggy Jarls of old
To launch their dragons on the unknown sea:
Such as kept strong the sinews of the sword,
The proud, hot blood of battle, — welcome made
The headsman's axe, the rack, the martyr-fire,
The ignominious cord,
When but to yield, had pomps and honors laid
On heads that moulder in ignoble mire.

V.

Night is the summer when the soul grows ripe
With Life's full harvest: of her myriad suns,
Thou dost not gild the quiet herdsman's pipe,
Nor royal state, that royal action shuns.
But in the noontide of thy ruddy stars
Thrive strength, and daring, and the blood whence springs
The Heraclidean seed of heroes; then
Were sundered Gaza's bars;
Then, 'mid the smitten Hydra's loosened rings,
His slayer rested, in the Lernean fen.

VI.

Thine is the subtle element that turns
  To fearless act the impulse of the hour, —
The secret fire, whose flash electric burns
  To every source of passion and of power.
Therefore I hail thee, on thy glittering track:
  Therefore I watch thee, when the night grows
      dark,
Slow-rising, front Orion's sword along
      The starry zodiac,
  And from thy mystic beam demand a spark
To warm my soul with more heroic song.

THE ODALISQUE.

In marble shells the fountain splashes ;
  Its falling spray is turned to stars,
When some light wind its pinion dashes
  Against thy gilded lattice-bars.
Around the shafts, in breathing cluster,
  The roses of Damascus run,
And through the summer's moons of lustre
  The tulip's goblet drinks the sun.

The day, through shadowy arches fainting,
  Reveals the garden's burst of bloom,
With lights of shifting iris painting
  The jasper pavement of thy room :
Enroofed with palm and laurel bowers,
  Thou seest, beyond, the cool kiosk,
And far away the pencilled towers
  That shoot from many a stately mosque.

Thou hast no world beyond the chamber
  Whose inlaid marbles mock the flowers,
Where burns thy lord's chibouk of amber,
  To charm the languid evening hours;
Where sounds the lute's impassioned yearning
  Through all enchanted tales of old,
And spicy cressets, dimly burning,
  Swing on their chains of Persian gold.

No more, in half-remembered vision,
  Thy distant childhood comes to view;
That star-like world of shapes Elysian
  Has faded from thy morning's blue:
The eastern winds that cross the Taurus
  Have now no voice of home beyond,
Where light waves foam in endless chorus
  Against the walls of Trebizond.

For thee the Past may never reckon
  Its hoard of saddening memories o'er,
Nor shapes from out the Future beckon
  To joys that only live in store.
Thy life is in the gorgeous Present,
  An Orient summer, warm and bright;
No gleam of beauty evanescent,
  But one long time of deep delight.

SORROWFUL MUSIC.

Give me music, or I die;
Music, wherein Sorrow's cry
Is a sweet, aerial sigh, —
Where Despair is harmony.

Give me music, such as winds
To the ambushed grief, and finds
Clews of soft-enticing sound,
Notes that soothe and cannot wound,
Leading with a tender care
Outward into brighter air:
Music which, with welcome pain,
Melted from the master's brain,
When his sorrow, freed from smart,
Laid its head upon his heart,
And the measure, broken, slow, —
Shed with tears in mingled flow, —

All its mighty secret spake
And it slept: it will not wake.

Give me music, sad and strong,
Drawn from deeper founts than Song;
More impassioned, full, and free
Than the Poet's numbers be:
Music which can master thee,
Stern enchantress, Memory!
Piercing through the gloomy stress
Of thy gathered bitterness,
As the summer lightnings play
Through a cloud's edge far away.

Give me music, I am dumb;
Choked with tears that never come.
Give me music; sigh or word
Such a sorrow never stirred,—
Sorrow that with blinding pain
Lies like fire on heart and brain.
Earth and Heaven bring no relief;
I am dumb; this weight of grief
Locks my lips; I cannot cry:
Give me music, or I die.

THE TULIP-TREE.

Now my blood, with long-forgotten fleetness,
  Bounds again to Boyhood's blithest tune,
While I drink a life of brimming sweetness
  From the glory of the breezy June.
Far above, the fields of ether brighten;
  Forest leaves are twinkling in their glee;
And the daisy's snows around me whiten,
  Drifted down the sloping lea!

On the hills he standeth as a tower,
  Shining in the morn, — the Tulip-Tree!
On his rounded turrets beats the shower,
  While his emerald flags are flapping free:
But when Summer, 'mid her harvests standing,
  Pours to him the sun's unmingled wine,
O'er his branches, all at once expanding,
  How the starry blossoms shine!

Through the glossy leaves they burn, unfolded,
  Like the fiery-breasted oriole,—
Filled with sweetness, as a thought new moulded
  Into being by a poet's soul!
Violet hills, against the sunrise lying,
  See them kindle when the stars grow pale,
And their lips, unclosed in balmy sighing,
  Sweeten all the morning gale.

Then all day, in every opening chalice,
  Drains their honey-drops the revelling bee,
Till the dove-winged Sleep makes thee her palace,
  Filled with song-like murmurs, Tulip-Tree!
In thine arms are rocked the dreams enchanted
  Which in Childhood's heart their dwelling made;
Dreams, whose glory to my brain is granted,
  When I lie amid thy shade.

Now, while Earth's full heart is throbbing over
  With its wealth of light and life and joy,
Who can feel how later years shall cover
  With their blight the visions of the boy?
Who can see the shadows downward darken,
  While the splendid morning bids aspire,
Or the turf upon his coffin hearken,
  When his pulses leap with fire!

Wind of June, that sweep'st the rolling meadow,
  Thou shalt wail in branches rough and bare,
While the tree, o'erhung with storm and shadow,
  Writhes and creaks amid the gusty air.
All his leaves, like shields of fairies scattered,
  Then shall drop before the North-wind's spears,
And his limbs, by hail and tempest battered,
  Feel the weight of wintry years.

Yet, why cloud the rapture and the glory
  Of the Beautiful, bequeathed us now?
Why relinquish all the Summer's story,
  Calling up the bleak autumnal bough?
Let thy blossoms in the morning brighten,
  Happy heart, as doth the Tulip-Tree,
While the daisy's snows around us whiten,
  Drifted down the sloping lea!

AUTUMNAL VESPERS.

THE clarion Wind, that blew so loud at morn,
Whirling a thousand leaves from every bough
Of the purple woods, has not a whisper now;
Hushed on the uplands is the huntsman's horn,
And huskers whistling round the tented corn:
The snug warm cricket lets his clock run down,
Scared by the chill, sad hour that makes forlorn
The Autumn's gold and brown.

The light is dying out on field and wold;
The life is dying in the leaves and grass.
The World's last breath no longer dims the glass
Of waning sunset, yellow, pale, and cold.
His genial pulse, which Summer made so bold,
Has ceased. Haste, Night, and spread thy decent pall!
The silent, stiffening Frost makes havoc: fold
The darkness over all!

The light is dying out o'er all the land,
  And in my heart the light is dying. She,
  My life's best life, is fading silently
From Earth, from me, and from the dreams we planned,
Since first Love led us with his beaming hand
  From hope to hope, yet kept his crown in store.
The light is dying out o'er all the land:
    To me it comes no more.

The blossom of my heart, she shrinks away,
  Stricken with deadly blight: more wan and weak
  Her love replies in blanching lip and cheek,
And gentler in her dear eyes, day by day.
God, in Thy mercy, bid the arm delay,
  Which through her being smites to dust my own!
Thou gav'st the seed thy sun and showers: why slay
    The blossoms yet unblown?

In vain, — in vain! God will not bid the Spring
  Replace with sudden green the Autumn's gold;
  And as the night-mists, gathering damp and cold,
Strike up the vales where water-courses sing,
Death's mist shall strike along her veins, and cling
  Thenceforth forever round her glorious frame:
For all her radiant presence, May shall bring
    A memory and a name.

What know the woods, that soon shall be so stark?
    What know the barren fields, the songless air,
    Locked in benumbing cold, of blooms more fair
In mornings ushered by the April lark?
Weak solace this, which Grief will never hark;
    Blind as a bud in stiff December's mail,
To lift her look beyond the frozen dark
        No memory can avail.

I never knew the autumnal eves could wear,
    With all their pomp, so drear a hue of Death;
    I never knew their still and solemn breath
Could rob the breaking heart of strength to bear,
Feeding the blank submission of despair.
    Yet, peace, sad soul! reproach and pity shine
Suffused through starry tears: bend thou in prayer,
        Rebuked by Love divine.

Our life is scarce the twinkle of a star
    In God's eternal day. Obscure and dim
    With mortal clouds, it yet may beam for Him,
And darkened here, shine fair to spheres afar.
I will be patient, lest my sorrow bar
    His grace and blessing, and I fall supine:
In my own hands my want and weakness are, —
        My strength, O God! in Thine.

ODE TO SHELLEY.

I.

Why art thou dead? Upon the hills once more
The golden mist of waning Autumn lies;
The slow-pulsed billows wash along the shore,
And phantom isles are floating in the skies.
They wait for thee: a spirit in the sand
Hushes, expectant for thy coming tread;
The light wind pants to lift thy trembling hair;
Inward, the silent land
Lies with its mournful woods; — why art thou dead,
When Earth demands that thou shalt call her fair?

II.

Why art thou dead ? I too demand thy song,
To speak the language yet denied to mine,
Twin-doomed with thee, to feel the scorn of Wrong,
To worship Beauty as a thing divine !
Thou art afar : wilt thou not soon return
To tell me that which thou hast never told ?
To clasp my throbbing hand, and, by the shore
Or dewy mountain-fern,
Pour out thy heart as to a friend of old,
Touched with a twilight sadness ? Nevermore.

III.

I could have told thee all the sylvan joy
Of trackless woods ; the meadows far apart,
Within whose fragrant grass, a lonely boy,
I thought of God ; the trumpet at my heart,
When on bleak mountains roared the midnight storm,
And I was bathed in lightning, broad and grand :
O, more than all, with soft and reverent breath
And forehead flushing warm,
I would have led thee through the summer land
Of early Love, and past my dreams of Death !

IV.

In thee, Immortal Brother! had I found
  That Voice of Earth, that fails my feebler lines:
The awful speech of Rome's sepulchral ground;
  The dusky hymn of Vallombrosa's pines!
From thee the noise of Ocean would have taken
  A grand defiance round the moveless shores,
And vocal grown the Mountain's silent head:
      Canst thou not yet awaken
  Beneath the funeral cypress? Earth implores
Thy presence for her son; — why art thou dead?

V.

I do but rave: for it is better thus.
  Were once thy starry nature given to mine,
In the one life which would encircle us
  My voice would melt, my soul be lost in thine.
Better to bear the far sublimer pain
  Of Thought that has not ripened into speech,
To hear in silence Truth and Beauty sing
      Divinely to the brain;
  For thus the Poet at the last shall reach
His own soul's voice, nor crave a brother's string.

SICILIAN WINE.

I'VE drunk Sicilia's crimson wine!
The blazing vintage pressed
From grapes on Etna's breast,
What time the mellowing autumn sun did shine:
I've drunk the wine!
I feel its blood divine
Poured on the sluggish tide of mine,
Till, kindling slow,
Its fountains glow
With the light that swims
On their trembling brims,
And a molten sunrise floods my limbs!

What do I here?
I've drunk the wine,
And lo! the bright blue heaven is clear
Above the ocean's bluer sphere,

Seen through the long arcades of pine,
Inwoven and arched with vine!
The glades are green below;
The temple shines afar;
Above, old Etna's snow
Sparkles with many an icy star:
I see the mountain and its marble wall,
Where gleaming waters fall
And voices call,
Singing and calling
Like chorals falling
Through pearly doors of some Olympian hall,
Where Love holds bacchanal.

Sicilian wine! Sicilian wine!
Summer, and Music, and Song divine
Are thine, — all thine!
A sweet wind over the roses plays;
The wild bee hums at my languid ear;
The mute-winged moth serenely strays
On the downy atmosphere,
Like hovering Sleep, that overweighs
My lids with his shadow, yet comes not near.
Who'll share with me this languor?
With me the juice of Etna sip?
Who press the goblet's lip

Refusing mine the while with love's enchanting anger?
Would I were young Adonis now!
With what an ardor bold
Within my arms I'd fold
Fair Aphrodite of Idalian mould,
And let the locks that hide her gleaming brow
Fall o'er my shoulder as she lay
With the fair swell of her immortal breast
Upon my bosom pressed,
Giving Olympian thrills to its enamoured clay!

Bacchus and Pan have fled:
No heavy Satyr crushes with his tread
The verdure of the meadow ground,
But in their stead
The Nymphs are leading a bewildering round,
Vivid and light, as o'er some flowering rise
A dance of butterflies,
Their tossing hair with slender lilies crowned,
And greener ivy than o'erran
The brows of Bacchus and the reed of Pan!

I faint, I die:
The flames expire,
That made my blood a fluid fire:
Steeped in delicious weariness I lie.

O, lay me in some pearlèd shell,
Soft-balanced on the rippling sea,
Where sweet, cheek-kissing airs may wave
Their fresh wings over me ;
Let me be wafted with the swell
Of Nereid voices; let no billow rave
To break the cool green crystal of the sea ;
For I will wander free
Past the blue islands and the fading shores,
To Calpè and the far Azores,
And still beyond, and wide away
Beneath the dazzling wings of tropic day,
Where, on unruffled seas,
Sleep the green isles of the Hesperides.

The Triton's trumpet calls:
I hear, I wake, I rise:
The sound peals up the skies,
And mellowed Echo falls
In answer back from Heaven's cerulean walls.
Give me the lyre that Orpheus played upon,
Or bright Hyperion, —
Nay, rather come, thou of the mighty bow,
Come thou below,
Leaving thy steeds unharnessed go!
Sing as thou wilt, my voice shall dare to follow,

And I will sun me in thine awful glow,
Divine Apollo!
Then thou thy lute shalt twine
With Bacchic tendrils of the glorious vine
That gave Sicilian wine:
And henceforth when the breezes run
Over its clusters, ripening in the sun,
The leaves shall still be playing,
Unto thy lute its melody repaying,
And I, that quaff, shall evermore be free
To mount thy car and ride the heavens with thee!

SUMMER'S BACCHANAL.

FILL the cup from some secretest fountain,
Under granite ledges, deep and low,
Where the crystal vintage of the mountain
Runs in foam from dazzling fields of snow!

Some lost stream, that in a woodland hollow
Coils, to sleep its weariness away,
Shut from prying stars, that fain would follow,
In the emerald glooms of hemlock spray.

Fill, dear friend, a goblet cool and sparkling
As the sunlight of October morns, —
Not for us the crimson wave, that darkling
Stains the lips of olden drinking-horns!

We will quaff, beneath the noontide glowing,
  Draughts of nectar, sweet as faery dew ;
Couched on ferny banks, where light airs blowing,
  Shake the leaves between us and the blue.

We will pledge, in breathless, long libation,
  All we have been, or have sworn to be, —
Fame, and Joy, and Love's dear adoration, —
  Summer's lusty bacchanals are we !

Fill again, and let our goblets, clashing,
  Stir the feathery ripples on the brim :
Let the light, within their bosoms flashing,
  Leap like youth to every idle limb !

Round the white roots of the fragrant lily,
  And the mossy hazels, purple-stained,
Once the music of these waters chilly
  Gave return for all the sweetness drained.

How that rare, delicious, woodland flavor
  Mocked my palate in the fever hours,
When I pined for springs of coolest savor,
  As the burning Earth for thunder-showers !

In the wave, which through my maddened dreaming
  Flowed to cheat me, fill the cups again!
Drink, dear friend, to life which is not seeming,—
  Fresh as this to manhood's heart and brain!

Fill, fill high! and while our goblets, ringing,
  Shine with vintage of the mountain-snow,
Youth shall bid his Fountain, blithely springing,
  Brim our souls to endless overflow!

STORM-LINES.

When the rains of November are dark on the hills, and
the pine-trees incessantly roar
To the sound of the wind-beaten crags, and the floods
that in foam through their black channels pour :

When the breaker-lined coast stretches dimly afar,
through the desolate waste of the gale,
And the clang of the sea-gull at nightfall is heard from
the deep, like a mariner's wail :

When the gray sky drops low, and the forest is bare,
and the laborer is housed from the storm,
And the world is a blank, save the light of his home
through the gust shining redly and warm : —

Go thou forth, if the brim of thy heart with its tropical
fulness of life overflow, —
If the sun of thy bliss in the zenith is hung, nor a
shadow reminds thee of woe!

Leave the home of thy love; leave thy labors of fame;
in the rain and the darkness go forth,
When the cold winds unpausingly wail as they drive
from the cheerless expanse of the North.

Thou shalt turn from the cup that was mantling before;
thou shalt hear the eternal despair
Of the hearts that endured and were broken at last,
from the hills and the sea and the air!

Thou shalt hear how the Earth, the maternal, laments
for the children she nurtured with tears, —
How the forest but deepens its wail and the breakers
their roar, with the march of the years!

Then the gleam of thy hearth-fire shall dwindle away,
and the lips of thy loved ones be still;
And thy soul shall lament in the moan of the storm,
sounding wide on the shelterless hill.

All the woes of existence shall stand at thy heart, and
    the sad eyes of myriads implore,
In the darkness and storm of their being, the ray,
    streaming out through thy radiant door.

Look again: how that star of thy Paradise dims,
    through the warm tears, unwittingly shed;—
Thou art man, and a sorrow so bitterly wrung never
    fell on the dust of the Dead!

Let the rain of the midnight beat cold on thy cheek,
    and the proud pulses chill in thy frame,
Till the love of thy bosom is grateful and sad, and
    thou turn'st from the mockery of Fame!

Take with humble acceptance the gifts of thy life; let
    thy joy touch the fountain of tears;
For the soul of the Earth, in endurance and pain, gath-
    ers promise of happier years!

THE TWO VISIONS.

THROUGH days of toil, through nightly fears,
A vision blessed my heart for years;
And so secure its features grew,
My heart believed the blessing true.

I saw her there, a household dove,
In consummated peace of love,
And sweeter joy and saintlier grace
Breathed o'er the beauty of her face:

The joy and grace of love at rest,
The fireside music of the breast,
When vain desires and restless schemes
Sleep, pillowed on our early dreams.

Nor her alone : beside her stood,
In gentler types, our love renewed ;
Our separate beings one, in Birth, —
The darling miracles of Earth.

The mother's smile, the children's kiss,
And home's serene, abounding bliss ;
The fruitage of a life that bore
But idle summer blooms before :

Such was the vision, far and sweet,
That, still beyond Time's lagging feet,
Lay glimmering in my heart for years,
Dim with the mist of happy tears.

That vision died, in drops of woe,
In blotting drops, dissolving slow :
Now, toiling day and sorrowing night,
Another vision fills my sight.

A cold mound in the winter snow ;
A colder heart at rest below ;
A life in utter loneness hurled,
And darkness over all the world.

THE LIFE OF EARTH.

THE breeze is blowing fresh and strong,
  The rocking shallop chafes its chain,
And the billows are breaking in swells of song,
  The rhythmical joy of the restless main.
A spirited stallion paws the sand;
  A hound is watching with eager eye;
The tramp of armies is felt in the land,
  And banners are dancing beneath the sky!

Let horns be heard in the gray ravine,
  And stormy songs from off the sea!
There's blood in my heart, where tears have been,
  And the blood of youth is warm and free.
Leave, weary Soul, the lifeless lore
  That kept these limbs in a slothful rust:
Lie down to rest on the quiet shore —
  The Dust has need of the life of dust!

Thou art weak and pallid, O form of flesh,
  Where the rubicund dawn once left its hue,
But the Earth shall bare her bosom afresh,
  And give thee the milk of manhood anew.
Thy locks shall toss on the mountain air,
  Thy limbs shall cool in the sparkling brine;
She will brace thy nerves with her forest-fare,
  And warm thy veins with generous wine!

Thy loins shall grow to a pard-like power
  On the windy slopes of the riven hills;
Thou shalt bare thy breast to the arrowy shower,
  And catch in thine arms the icy rills!
Thy vigorous blood shall exult the same,
  Though fevered cares in the spirit start,
As a pine, when the mountain is swathed in flame,
  Keeps green and fresh in his spicy heart.

Thou shalt go where the battle-clarions blare,
  As heroes went, ere the brain was lord;
Thine eye with the soldier's lust shall glare,
  Thy heart shall smite in the clanging sword.
The cannon will bellow thy mad desire,
  And the shock of combat thine arm employ,
Till the thews are steel, and the veins are fire,
  And death at last is a terrible joy!

Then tighten the girth and loosen the rein!
  Unleash the baying, impatient hound,
And deep in the surging and seething main
  Let every quivering oar be drowned.
We are free! we have quelled the tyrant Soul:
  We shall fill the world with our rebel mirth,
While the laughing vineyards crown the bowl
  That brims for us with the Life of Earth!

STORM SONG.

THE clouds are scudding across the moon,
A misty light is on the sea;
The wind in the shrouds has a wintry tune,
And the foam is flying free.

Brothers, a night of terror and gloom
Speaks in the cloud and gathering roar;
Thank God, He has given us broad sea-room,
A thousand miles from shore.

Down with the hatches on those who sleep!
The wild and whistling deck have we;
Good watch, my brothers, to-night we'll keep,
While the tempest is on the sea!

Though the rigging shriek in his terrible grip,
  And the naked spars be snapped away,
Lashed to the helm, we'll drive our ship
  In the teeth of the whelming spray!

Hark! how the surges o'erleap the deck!
  Hark! how the pitiless tempest raves!
Ah, daylight will look upon many a wreck
  Drifting over the desert waves.

Yet, courage, brothers! we trust the wave,
  With God above us, our guiding chart:
So, whether to harbor or ocean-grave,
  Be it still with a cheery heart!

SONG.

I PLUCKED for thee the wilding rose
 And wore it on my breast,
And there, till daylight's dusky close,
 Its silken cheek was pressed;
Its desert breath was sweeter far
 Than palace-rose could be,
Sweeter than all Earth's blossoms are,
 But that thou gav'st to me.

I kissed its leaves, in fond despite
 Of lips that failed my own,
And Love recalled that sacred night
 His blushing flower was blown.
I vowed, no rose should rival mine,
 Though withered now, and pale,
Till those are pluckéd, whose white buds twine
 Above thy bridal veil.

THE WAVES.

I.

CHILDREN are we
Of the restless sea,
Swelling in anger or sparkling in glee;
We follow our race,
In shifting chase,
Over the boundless ocean-space!
Who hath beheld where the race begun?
Who shall behold it run?
Who shall behold it run?

II.

When the smooth airs keep
Their noontide sleep,
We dimple the cheek of the dreaming deep;

When the rough winds come
From their cloudy home,
At the tap of the hurricane's thunder-drum,
Deep are the furrows of wrath we plough,
Ridging his darkened brow!
Ridging his darkened brow!

III.

Over us born,
The unclouded Morn
Trumpets her joy with the Triton's horn,
And sun and star
By the thousand are
Orbed in our glittering, near and far:
And the splendor of Heaven, the pomp of Day,
Shine in our laughing spray!
Shine in our laughing spray!

IV.

We murmur our spell
Over sand and shell;
We girdle the reef with a combing swell;

And bound in the vice
Of the Arctic ice,
We build us a palace of grand device,—
Walls of crystal and splintered spires,
Flashing with diamond fires!
Flashing with diamond fires!

V.

In the endless round
Of our motion and sound,
The fairest dwelling of Beauty is found,
And with voice of strange
And solemn change,
The elements speak in our world-wide range,
Harping the terror, the might, the mirth,
Sorrows and hopes of Earth!
Sorrows and hopes of Earth!

SONG.

From the bosom of ocean I seek thee,
  Thou lamp of my spirit afar,
As the seaman, adrift in the darkness,
  Looks up for the beam of his star;
And when on the moon-lighted water
  The spirits of solitude sleep,
My soul, in the light of thy beauty,
  Lies hushed as the waves of the deep.

As the shafts of the sunrise are broken
  Far over the glittering sea,
Thou hast dawned on the waves of my dreaming,
  And each thought has a sparkle of thee.
And though, with the white sail distended,
  I speed from the vanishing shore,
Thou wilt give to the silence of ocean
  The spell of thy beauty the more.

CRICKET SONG.

Welcome with thy clicking, cricket!
  Clicking songs of sober mirth;
Autumn, stripping field and thicket,
  Brings thee to my hearth,
Where thy clicking shrills and quickens,
While the mist of twilight thickens.

Lately, by the garden wicket,
  Where the thick grass grew unclipt,
And the rill beside thee, cricket,
  Silver-trickling slipt,
Thou, in midday's silent glitter,
Mocked the flickering linnet's twitter.

Now thou art, my cheerful cricket,
  Nimble quickener of my song;
Not a thought but thou shalt nick it
  In thy lowly tongue,

And my clock, the moments ticking,
Is thy constant clicking, clicking.

No annoy, good-humored cricket,
  With thy trills is ever blent;
Spleen of mine, how dost thou trick it
  To a calm content!
So, by thicket, hearth, or wicket,
Click thy little lifetime, cricket!

WORDSWORTH.

I SAW thee not, what time mine eyes beheld
Far-off Helvellyn skirt the misty sea,
When wild Manx waters foamed and tumbled free
Around my keel: I saw thee not, when swelled
Beyond Northumbrian moors the soft-blue line
Of mountain chains that look on Windermere;
Yet was it joy to know thy paths so near,
Thy voice on all those hills, O Bard divine!
But I shall see thee where thou sittest now,
Musing, uplift o'er deeps of diamond air,
And I shall feel the splendor of thy brow
Thrown on the scanty wreath that binds my hair,
As, looking down benignly on my place,
Thou read'st the reverence in my lifted face.

SONNET.

TO G. H. B.

YOU comfort me as one that, knowing Fate,
Would paint her visage kinder than you deem;
You say, my only bliss that is no dream
She clouds, but makes not wholly desolate.
Ah, Friend! your heart speaks words of little weight
To veil that sadder knowledge, learned in song,
And 'gainst your solace Grief has made me strong:
The Gods are jealous of our low estate;
They give not Fame to Love, nor Love to Fame;
Power cannot taste the joy the humbler share,
Nor holy Beauty breathe in Luxury's air,
And all in darkness Genius feeds his flame.
We build and build, poor fools! and all the while
Some Demon works unseen, and saps the pile.

CALIFORNIAN BALLADS AND POEMS.

MANUELA.

FROM the doorway, Manuela, in the sheeny April
morn,
Southward looks, along the valley, over leagues of
gleaming corn;
Where the mountain's misty rampart like the wall of
Eden towers,
And the isles of oak are sleeping on a painted sea of
flowers.

All the air is full of music, for the winter rains are
o'er,
And the noisy magpies chatter from the budding syca-
more;
Blithely frisk unnumbered squirrels, over all the grassy
slope;
Where the airy summits brighten, nimbly leaps the
antelope.

Gentle eyes of Manuela! tell me wherefore do ye
rest
On the oak's enchanted islands and the flowery ocean's
breast?
Tell me wherefore, down the valley, ye have traced
the highway's mark
Far beyond the belts of timber, to the mountain-shadows dark?

Ah, the fragrant bay may blossom and the sprouting
verdure shine
With the tears of amber dropping from the tassels of
the pine,
And the morning's breath of balsam lightly brush her
sunny cheek,—
Little recketh Manuela of the tales of Spring they
speak.

When the Summer's burning solstice on the mountain-harvests glowed,
She had watched a gallant horseman riding down the
valley road;
Many times she saw him turning, looking back with
parting thrills,
Till amid her tears she lost him, in the shadow of the
hills.

Ere the cloudless moons were over, he had passed the
Desert's sand,
Crossed the rushing Colorado and the wild Apachè
Land,
And his laden mules were driven, when the time of
rains began,
With the traders of Chihuahua, to the Fair of San
Juan.

Therefore watches Manuela, — therefore lightly doth
she start,
When the sound of distant footsteps seems the beating
of her heart;
Not a wind the green oak rustles or the redwood
branches stirs,
But she hears the silver jingle of his ringing bit and
spurs.

Often, out the hazy distance, come the horsemen, day
by day,
But they come not as Bernardo, — she can see it, far
away;
Well she knows the airy gallop of his mettled ala-
zàn,
Light as any antelope upon the Hills of Gavilàn.

She would know him 'mid a thousand, by his free and
gallant air;
By the featly-knit sarápè, such as wealthy traders
wear;
By his broidered calzoneros and his saddle, gayly
spread,
With its cantle rimmed with silver, and its horn a lion's
head.

None like him the light riáta on the maddened bull can
throw;
None amid the mountain-cañons track like him the
stealthy doe;
And at all the Mission festals, few indeed the revellers
are
Who can dance with him the jota, touch with him the
gay guitar.

He has said to Manuela, and the echoes linger
still
In the cloisters of her bosom, with a secret, tender
thrill,
When the bay again has blossomed, and the valley
stands in corn,
Shall the bells of Santa Clara usher in the wedding
morn.

He has pictured the procession, all in holiday attire,
And the laugh of bridal gladness, when they see the distant spire;
Then their love shall kindle newly, and the world be doubly fair
In the cool, delicious crystal of the summer morning air.

Tender eyes of Manuela! what has dimmed your lustrous beam?
'Tis a tear that falls to glitter on the casket of her dream.
Ah, the eye of Love must brighten, if its watches would be true,
For the star is falsely mirrored in the rose's drop of dew!

But her eager eyes rekindle, and her breathless bosom thrills,
As she sees a horseman moving in the shadow of the hills:
Now in love and fond thanksgiving they may loose their pearly tides,—
'Tis the alazàn that gallops, 'tis Bernardo's self that rides!

THE FIGHT OF PASO DEL MAR.

Gusty and raw was the morning,
  A fog hung over the seas,
And its gray skirts, rolling inland,
  Were torn by the mountain trees;
No sound was heard but the dashing
  Of waves on the sandy bar,
When Pablo of San Diego
  Rode down to the Paso del Mar.

The pescadòr, out in his shallop,
  Gathering his harvest so wide,
Sees the dim bulk of the headland
  Loom over the waste of the tide;
He sees, like a white thread, the pathway
  Wind round on the terrible wall,
Where the faint, moving speck of the rider
  Seems hovering close to its fall.

Stout Pablo of San Diego
  Rode down from the hills behind ;
With the bells on his gray mule tinkling
  He sang through the fog and wind.
Under his thick, misted eyebrows,
  Twinkled his eye like a star,
And fiercer he sang as the sea-winds
  Drove cold on the Paso del Mar.

Now Bernal, the herdsman of Chino,
  Had travelled the shore since dawn,
Leaving the ranches behind him —
  Good reason had he to be gone !
The blood was still red on his dagger,
  The fury was hot in his brain,
And the chill, driving scud of the breakers
  Beat thick on his forehead in vain.

With his poncho wrapped gloomily round him,
  He mounted the dizzying road,
And the chasms and steeps of the headland
  Were slippery and wet, as he trod :
Wild swept the wind of the ocean,
  Rolling the fog from afar,
When near him a mule-bell came tinkling,
  Midway on the Paso del Mar.

"Back!" shouted Bernal, full fiercely,
  And "Back!" shouted Pablo, in wrath,
As his mule halted, startled and shrinking,
  On the perilous line of the path.
The roar of devouring surges
  Came up from the breakers' hoarse war;
And "Back, or you perish!" cried Bernal,
  "I turn not on Paso del Mar!"

The gray mule stood firm as the headland:
  He clutched at the jingling rein,
When Pablo rose up in his saddle
  And smote till he dropped it again.
A wild oath of passion swore Bernal,
  And brandished his dagger, still red,
While fiercely stout Pablo leaned forward,
  And fought o'er his trusty mule's head.

They fought till the black wall below them
  Shone red through the misty blast;
Stout Plablo then struck, leaning farther,
  The broad breast of Bernal at last.
And, frenzied with pain, the swart herdsman
  Closed on him with terrible strength,
And jerked him, despite of his struggles,
  Down from the saddle at length.

They grappled with desperate madness,
  On the slippery edge of the wall;
They swayed on the brink, and together
  Reeled out to the rush of the fall.
A cry of the wildest death-anguish
  Rang faint through the mist afar,
And the riderless mule went homeward
  From the fight of the Paso del Mar.

THE PINE FOREST OF MONTEREY.

What point of Time, unchronicled, and dim
As yon gray mist that canopies your heads,
Took from the greedy wave and gave the sun
Your dwelling-place, ye gaunt and hoary Pines?
When, from the barren bosoms of the hills,
With scanty nurture, did ye slowly climb,
Of these remote and latest-fashioned shores
The first-born forest? Titans gnarled and rough,
Such as from out subsiding Chaos grew
To clothe the cold loins of the savage earth,
What fresh commixture of the elements,
What earliest thrill of life, the stubborn soil
Slow-mastering, engendered ye to give
The hills a mantle and the wind a voice?
Along the shore ye lift your rugged arms,
Blackened with many fires, and with hoarse chant —

Unlike the fibrous lute your co-mates touch
In elder regions — fill the awful stops
Between the crashing cataracts of the surf.
Have ye no tongue, in all your sea of sound,
To syllable the secret, — no still voice
To give your airy myths a shadowy form,
And make us of lost centuries of lore
The rich inheritors?

The sea-winds pluck
Your mossy beards, and gathering as they sweep,
Vex your high heads, and with your sinewy arms
Grapple and toil in vain. A deeper roar,
Sullen and cold, and rousing into spells
Of stormy volume, is your sole reply.
Anchored in firm-set rock, ye ride the blast.
And from the promontory's utmost verge
Make signal o'er the waters. So ye stood,
When, like a star, behind the lonely sea,
Far shone the white speck of Grijalva's sail;
And when, through driving fog, the breaker's sound
Frighted Otondo's men, your spicy breath
Played as in welcome round their rusty helms,
And backward from its staff shook out the folds
Of Spain's emblazoned banner.

Ancient Pines,
Ye bear no record of the years of man.
Spring is your sole historian, — Spring, that paints
These savage shores with hues of Paradise ;
That decks your branches with a fresher green,
And through your lonely, far cañadas pours
Her floods of bloom, rivers of opal dye
That wander down to lakes and widening seas
Of blossom and of fragrance, — laughing Spring,
That with her wanton blood refills your veins,
And weds ye to your juicy youth again
With a new ring, the while your rifted bark
Drops odorous tears. Your knotty fibres yield
To the light touch of her unfailing pen,
As freely as the lupin's violet cup.
Ye keep, close-locked, the memories of her stay,
As in their shells the avelonès keep
Morn's rosy flush and moonlight's pearly glow.
The wild north-west, that from Alaska sweeps,
To drown Point Lobos with the icy scud
And white sea-foam, may rend your boughs and leave
Their blasted antlers tossing in the gale ;
Your steadfast hearts are mailed against the shock,
And on their annual tablets nought inscribe
Of such rude visitation. Ye are still
The simple children of a guiltless soil,

And in your natures show the sturdy grain
That passion cannot jar, nor force relax,
Nor aught but sweet and kindly airs compel
To gentler mood. No disappointed heart
Has sighed its bitterness beneath your shade;
No angry spirit ever came to make
Your silence its confessional; no voice,
Grown harsh in Crime's great market-place, the world,
Tainted with blasphemy your evening hush
And aromatic air. The deer alone, —
The ambushed hunter that brings down the deer, —
The fisher wandering on the misty shore
To watch sea-lions wallow in the flood, —
The shout, the sound of hoofs that chase and fly,
When swift vaqueros, dashing through the herds,
Ride down the angry bull, — perchance, the song
Some Indian heired of long-forgotten sires, —
Disturb your solemn chorus.

Stately Pines,
But few more years around the promontory
Your chant will meet the thunders of the sea.
No more, a barrier to the encroaching sand,
Against the surf ye'll stretch defiant arm,
Though with its onset and besieging shock
Your firm knees tremble. Never more the wind

Shall pipe shrill music through your mossy beards,
Nor sunset's yellow blaze athwart your heads
Crown all the hills with gold. Your race is past:
The mystic cycle, whose unnoted birth
Coeval was with yours, has run its sands,
And other footsteps from these changing shores
Frighten its haunting Spirit. Men will come
To vex your quiet with the din of toil;
The smoky volumes of the forge will stain
This pure, sweet air; loud keels will ride the sea,
Dashing its glittering sapphire into foam;
Through all her green cañadas Spring will seek
Her lavish blooms in vain, and clasping ye,
O mournful Pines, within her glowing arms,
Will weep soft rains to find ye fallen low.
Fall, therefore, yielding to the fiat! Fall,
Ere the maturing soil, whose first dull life
Fed your belated germs, be rent and seamed!
Fall, like the chiefs ye sheltered, stern, unbent,
Your gray beards hiding memorable scars!
The winds will mourn ye, and the barren hills
Whose breast ye clothed; and when the pauses come
Between the crashing cataracts of the surf,
A funeral silence, terrible, profound,
Will make sad answer to the listening sea.

EL CANELO.

I.

Now saddle El Canelo! — the freshening wind of
morn,
Down in the flowery vega, is stirring through the
corn;
The thin smoke of the ranches grows red with coming
day,
And the steed is fiercely stamping, in haste to be
away.

II.

My glossy-limbed Canelo, thy neck is curved in
pride,
Thy slender ears pricked forward, thy nostril straining
wide;

And as thy quick neigh greets me, and I catch thee by
the mane,
I'm off with the winds of morning — the chieftain of
the plain!

III.

I feel the swift air whirring, and see along our
track,
From the flinty-paved sierra, the sparks go streaming
back;
And I clutch my rifle closer, as we sweep the dark
defile,
Where the red guerillas ambush for many a lonely
mile.

IV.

They reach not El Canelo; with the swiftness of a
dream
We've passed the bleak Nevada, and San Fernando's
stream;
But where, on sweeping gallop, my bullet backward
sped,
The keen-eyed mountain vultures will wheel above the
dead.

V.

On! on, my brave Canelo! we've dashed the sand and snow
From peaks upholding heaven, from deserts far below —
We've thundered through the forest, while the crackling branches rang,
And trooping elks, affrighted, from lair and covert sprang.

VI.

We've swum the swollen torrent — we've distanced in the race
The baying wolves of Pinos, that panted with the chase;
And still thy mane streams backward, at every thrilling bound,
And still thy measured hoof-stroke beats with its morning sound!

VII.

The seaward winds are wailing through Santa Barbara's pines,
And like a sheathless sabre, the far Pacific shines;

Hold to thy speed, my arrow! at nightfall thou shalt
lave
Thy hot and smoking haunches beneath his silver
wave!

VIII.

My head upon thy shoulder, along the sloping
sand
We'll sleep as trusty brothers, from out the mountain
land;
The pines will sound in answer to the surges on the
shore,
And in our dreams, Canelo, we'll make the journey
o'er.

THE EAGLE HUNTER.

STORM and rain are on the mountains,
And the falling torrents thunder,
And the black and driving shadows
Make a night along the plain:
Now the herds are grouped for shelter,
And the herdsmen wind their lassos,
Towards the distant hacienda
Speeding homeward through the rain.

From the icy Cordilleras
Crashing leap the avalanches,
By the hands of mining waters
Loosened from their lofty hold;
And the mountain sheep are scattered
By the firs and larches falling,
And the wild wolves howling gather
In the caverns dark and cold.

On the lofty summit, beaten
By the wintry sleet, I wander,
For I seek the monarch eagle
        In his eyrie of the rock;
And I shout in exultation,
When his gray wing on the darkness
Of the cloud above me flashes,
        Wheeling downward to the shock!

From his wing I rob the plumage,
And it crowns me like a chieftain;
At my belt his talons rattle,
        Like the scales of olden mail:
Never win the Yuma hunters
Such a trophy on their deserts,
Or the fiery-eyed Apache
        In the Colorado's vale!

I pursue a nobler quarry,
And my home is far above them,
Where the cradles of the rivers
        Have been hollowed in the snow.
And I drink their crystal sources,
Where the Bravo and the Gila
To their thousand miles of travel
        Plunging down the cañons go!

In the meeting of the thunders,
When the solid crags are shivered,
Firm and fearless and rejoicing
        On the lonely peaks I stand ;
For my foot has learned the fleetness
Of the ibex on the ridges,
And my voice the stormy music
        Of the mighty Mountain Land.

THE SUMMER CAMP.

Here slacken rein; here let the dusty mules
Unsaddled graze! The shadows of the oaks
Are on our brows, and through their knotted boles
We see the blue round of the boundless plain
Vanish in glimmering heat: these aged oaks,
The island speck that beckoned us afar
Over the burning level, — as we came,
Spreading to shore and cape, and bays that ran
To leafy headlands, balanced on the haze,
Faint and receding as a cloud in air.

The mules may roam unsaddled: we will lie
Beneath the mighty trees, whose shade, like dew
Poured from the urns of Twilight, dries the sweat
Of sunburnt brows, and on the heavy lid
And heated eyeball sheds a balm, than sleep

Far sweeter. We have done with travel,— we
Are weary now, who never dreamed of Rest,
For until now did never Rest unbar
Her palace-doors, nor until now our ears
The silence drink, beyond all melodies
Of all imagined sound, that wraps her realm.
Here, where the desolating centuries
Have left no mark; where noises never came
From the far world of battle and of toil;
Where God looks down and sends no thunderbolt
To smite a human wrong, for all is good,
She finds a refuge. We will dwell with her.

No more of travel, where the flaming sword
Of the great sun divides the heavens; no more
Of climbing over jutty steeps that swim
In driving sea-mist, where the stunted tree
Slants inland, mimicking the stress of winds
When wind is none; of plain and steaming marsh
Where the dry bulrush crackles in the heat;
Of camps by starlight in the columned vault
Of sycamores, and the red, dancing fires
That build a leafy arch, efface and build,
And sink at last, to let the stars peep through;
Of cañons grown with pine and folded deep
In golden mountain-sides; of airy sweeps

Of mighty landscape, lying all alone
Like some deserted world. They tempt no more.
It is enough that such things were : too blest,
O comrades mine, to lie in Summer's arms,
Lodged in her Camp of Rest, we will not dream
That they may vex us more.

The sun goes down :
The dun mules wander idly : motionless
Beneath the stars, the heavy foliage lifts
Its rich, round masses, silent as a cloud
That sleeps at midday on a mountain peak.
All through the long, delicious night no stir
Is in the leaves ; spangled with broken gleams,
Before the pining Moon — that fain would drop
Into the lap of this deep quiet — swerve
Eastward the shadows : Day comes on again.
Where is the life we led ? Whither hath fled
The turbulent stream that brought us hither ? How,
So full of sound, so lately dancing down
The mountains, turbid, fretted into foam, —
How has it slipped, with scarce a gurgling coil,
Into this calm transparence, noise or wind
Hath ruffled never ? Ages past, perchance,
Such wild turmoil was ours, or did some Dream
Malign, that last night nestled in the oak,

Whisper our ears, when not a star could see?
Give o'er the fruitless doubt: we will not waste
One thought of rest, nor spill one radiant drop
From the full goblet of this summer balm.

Day after day the mellow sun slides o'er,
Night after night the mellow moon. The clouds
Are laid, enchanted: soft and bare, the heavens
Fold to their breast the dozing Earth, that lies
In languor of deep bliss. At times, a breath,
Remnant of gales far off, forgotten now,
Rustles the never-fading leaves, then drops
Affrighted into silence. Near a slough
Of dark, still water, in the early morn
The shy coyotas prowl, or trooping elk
From the close covert of the bulrush-fields
Their dewy antlers toss: nor other sight,
Save when the falcon, poised on wheeling wings,
His bright eye on the burrowing coney, cuts
His arrowy plunge. Along the distant trail,
Dim with the heat, sometimes the miners go
Bearded and rough, the swart Sonorians drive
Their laden asses, or vaqueros whirl
The lasso's coil and carol many a song,
Native to Spanish hills. As when we lie
On the soft brink of Sleep, not pillowed quite

To blest forgetfulness, some dim array
Of masking forms in long procession comes,
A sweet disturbance to the poppied sense,
That will not cease, but gently holds it back
From slumber's haven, so their figures pass,
With such disturbance cloud the blessèd calm,
And hold our beings, ready to slip forth
O'er unmolested seas, still rocking near
The coasts of Action.

Other dreams are ours,
Of shocks that were, or seemed ; whereof our souls
Feel the subsiding lapse, as feels the sand
Of tropic island-shores the dying pulse
Of storms that racked the Northern sea. My Soul,
I do believe that thou hast toiled and striven,
And hoped and suffered wrong. I do believe
Great aims were thine, deep loves and fiery hates,
And though I may have lain a thousand years
Beneath these Oaks, the baffled trust of Youth,
Thy first keen sorrow, brings a gentle pang
To temper joy. Nor will the joy I drank
To wild intoxication, quit my heart :
It was no dream that still has power to droop
The soft-suffusing lid, and lift desire
Beyond this rapt repose. No dream, dear love !
For thou art with me in our Camp of Peace.

O Friend, whose history is writ in deeds
That make your life a marvel, come no gleams
Of past adventure, echoes of old storms,
And Battle's tingling hum of flying shot,
To touch your easy blood and tempt you o'er
The round of yon blue plain? Or have they lost,
Heroic days, the virtue which the heart
That did their hest rejoicing, proved so high?
Back through the long, long cycles of our rest
Your memory travels: through this hush you hear
The Gila's dashing, feel the yawning jaws
Of black volcanic gorges close you in
On waste and awful tracts of wilderness,
Which other than the eagle's cry, or bleat
Of mountain-goat, hear not: the scorching sand
Eddies around the tracks your fainting mules
Leave in the desert: thorn and cactus pierce
Your bleeding limbs, and stiff with raging thirst
Your tongue forgets its office. Leave untried
That cruel trail, and leave the wintry hills
And leave the tossing sea! The Summer here
Builds us a tent of everlasting calm.

How shall we wholly sink our lives in thee,
Thrice-blessèd Deep? O many-natured Soul,
Chameleon-like, that, steeped in every phase

Of wide existence, tak'st the hue of each,
Here with the silent Oaks and azure Air
Incorporate grow! Here loosen one by one
Thy vexing memories, burdens of the Past,
Till all unrest be laid, and strong Desire
Sleeps on his nerveless arm. Content to find
In liberal Peace thy being's high result
And crown of aspiration, gather all
The dreams of sense, the reachings of the mind
For ampler issues and dominion vain,
To fold them on her bosom, happier there
Than in exultant action: as a child
Forgets his meadow butterflies and flowers,
Upon his mother's breast.

It may not be.
Not in this Camp, in these enchanted Trees,
But in ourselves, must lodge the calm we seek,
Ere we can fix it here. We cannot take
From outward nature power to snap the curse
Which clothed our birth; and though 'twere easier
This hour to die than yield the blessèd cup
Wherefrom our hearts divinest comfort draw,
It clothes us yet, and yet shall drive us forth
To breast the world. Then come: we will not bide
To tempt a ruin to this paradise,

Fulfilling Destiny. A mighty wind
Would gather on the plain, a cloud arise
To blot the sky, with thunder in its heart,
And the black column of the whirlwind spin
Out of the cloud, straight downward to this grove,
Take by their heads the shuddering trees, and wrench
With fearful clamor, limb from limb, till Rest
Should flee forever. Rather set at once
Our faces toward the noisy world again,
And gird our loins for action. Let us go!

THE BISON TRACK.

I.

STRIKE the tent! the sun has risen; not a vapor streaks
the dawn,
And the frosted prairie brightens to the westward, far
and wan:
Prime afresh the trusty rifle — sharpen well the hunting
spear —
For the frozen sod is trembling, and a noise of hoofs I
hear!

II.

Fiercely stamp the tethered horses, as they snuff the
morning's fire;
Their impatient heads are tossing, and they neigh with
keen desire.

Strike the tent! the saddles wait us — let the bridle-
reins be slack,
For the prairie's distant thunder has betrayed the bi-
son's track.

III.

See! a dusky line approaches: hark, the onward-sur-
ging roar,
Like the din of wintry breakers on a sounding wall of
shore!
Dust and sand behind them whirling, snort the foremost
of the van,
And their stubborn horns are clashing through the
crowded caravan.

IV.

Now the storm is down upon us: let the maddened
horses go!
We shall ride the living whirlwind, though a hundred
leagues it blow!
Though the cloudy manes should thicken, and the red
eyes' angry glare
Lighten round us as we gallop through the sand and
rushing air!

V.

Myriad hoofs will scar the prairie, in our wild, resistless race,
And a sound, like mighty waters, thunder down the desert space:
Yet the rein may not be tightened, nor the rider's eye look back —
Death to him whose speed should slacken, on the maddened bison's track!

VI.

Now the trampling herds are threaded, and the chase is close and warm
For the giant bull that gallops in the edges of the storm:
Swiftly hurl the whizzing lasso — swing your rifles as we run:
See! the dust is red behind him — shout, my comrades, he is won!

VII.

Look not on him as he staggers — 'tis the last shot he will need!
More shall fall, among his fellows, ere we run the mad stampede —

Ere we stem the brinded breakers, while the wolves, a
hungry pack,
Howl around each grim-eyed carcass, on the bloody
Bison Track !

RHYMES OF TRAVEL, AND EARLY POEMS.

THE TOMB OF CHARLEMAGNE.

I STOOD in that cathedral old, the work of kingly power,
That from the clustered roofs of Aix lifts up its mouldering tower,
And, like a legend strange and rude, speaks of an earlier day —
Of saint and knight, the tourney's pomp and the Minnesinger's lay!

Above me rose the pillared dome, with many a statue grim,
And through the chancel-oriel came a splendor soft and dim,
Till dusky shrine and painting old glowed in the lustre wan:
Below me was a marble slab — the Tomb of Charlemagne.

A burst of organ-music rang so grandly, sadly slow,
It seemed a requiem thundered o'er the dead who slept below;
And with the sound came thronging round the stern men of that time,
When best was he who bravest fought, and cowardice was crime.

I thought upon the day when he, whose dust I stood upon,
Ruled with a monarch's boundless right the kingdoms he had won —
When rose the broad Alps in his realm, and roared the Baltic's wave;
And now — the lowest serf might stand, unheeded, on his grave.

And ruthless hands despoiled his dust, attired in regal pride,
The crown upon his crumbled brows, and *Joyeuse* by his side —
Whose rusted blade, at Ronçeval, flamed in the hero's hand
In answer to the silver horn of the Paladin, Rolànd.

I stood on that neglected stone, thrilled with the glorious sound,
While bowed at many a holier shrine the worshippers around —
And through the cloud of incense-smoke burned many a taper dim,
And priestly stoles went sweeping by — I could but think of him!

I saw the boy with yellow locks, crowned at St. Deny's shrine;
The emperor in his purple cloak, the lord of all the Rhine;
The conqueror of a thousand foes, in battle stern and hard;
The widowed mourner at thy tomb, O fairest Hildegarde!

Long pealed the music of the choir through chancel-arch and nave,
As, lost in those old memories, I stood upon his grave;
And when the morning anthem ceased, and solemn mass began,
I left that minster gray and old — the Tomb of Charlemagne.

Aix-la-Chapelle, 1844.

THE WAYSIDE DREAM.

THE deep and lordly Danube
  Goes winding far below;
I see the white-walled hamlets
  Amid his vineyards glow,
And southward, through the ether, shine
  The Styrian hills of snow.

O'er many a league of landscape
  Sleeps the warm haze of noon;
The wooing winds come freighted
  With messages of June,
And down among the corn and flowers
  I hear the water's tune.

The meadow-lark is singing,
  As if it still were morn;

Within the dark pine-forest
  The hunter winds his horn,
And the cuckoo's shy, complaining note
  Mocks the maidens in the corn.

I watch the cloud-armada
  Go sailing up the sky,
Lulled by the murmuring mountain grass
  Upon whose bed I lie,
And the faint sound of noonday chimes
  That in the distance die.

A warm and drowsy sweetness
  Is stealing o'er my brain;
I see no more the Danube
  Sweep through his royal plain;
I hear no more the peasant girls
  Singing amid the grain.

Soft, silvery wings, a moment
  Have swept across my brow:
Again I hear the water,
  But its voice is sweeter now,
And the mocking-bird and oriole
  Are singing on the bough!

The elm and linden branches
  Droop close and dark o'erhead,
And the foaming forest brooklet
  Leaps down its rocky bed:
Be still, my heart! the seas are passed —
  The paths of home I tread!

The showers of creamy blossoms
  Are on the linden spray,
And down the clover meadow
  They heap the scented hay,
And glad winds toss the forest leaves,
  All the bright summer day.

Old playmates! bid me welcome
  Amid your brother-band;
Give me the old affection —
  The glowing grasp of hand!
I seek no more the realms of old —
  Here is my Fatherland.

Come hither, gentle maiden,
  Who weep'st in tender joy!
The rapture of thy presence
  Repays the world's annoy,

And calms the wild and ardent heart
  Which warms the wandering boy.

In many a mountain fastness,
  By many a river's foam,
And through the gorgeous cities,
  'Twas loneliness to roam;
For the sweetest music in my heart
  Was the olden songs of home.

Ah, glen and grove are vanished,
  And friends have faded now!
The balmy Styrian breezes
  Are blowing on my brow,
And sounds again the cuckoo's call
  From the forest's inmost bough.

Fled is that happy vision —
  The gates of slumber fold;
I rise and journey onward
  Through valleys green and old,
Where the far, white Alps announce the morn,
  And keep the sunset's gold.

UPPER AUSTRIA, 1845.

STEYERMARK.

In Steyermark — green Steyermark,
The fields are bright and the forests dark —
Bright with the maids that bind the sheaves,
Dark with the arches of whispering leaves!
Voices and streams and sweet bells chime
Over the land, in the harvest-time,
And the blithest songs of the finch and lark
Are heard in the orchards of Steyermark.

In Steyermark — old Steyermark,
The mountain summits are white and stark;
The rough winds furrow their trackless snow,
But the mirrors of crystal are smooth below;
The stormy Danube clasps the wave
That downward sweeps with the Drave and Save,
And the Euxine is whitened with many a bark,
Freighted with ores of Steyermark!

In Steyermark — rough Steyermark,
The anvils ring from dawn till dark ;
The molten streams of the furnace glare,
Blurring with crimson the midnight air ;
The lusty voices of forgemen chord,
Chanting the ballad of Siegfried's Sword,
While the hammers swung by their arms so stark
Strike to the music of Steyermark !

In Steyermark — dear Steyermark,
Each heart is light as the morning lark :
There men are framed in the manly mould
Of their stalwart sires, of the times of old,
And the sunny blue of the Styrian sky
Grows soft in the timid maiden's eye,
When love descends with the twilight dark,
In the beechen groves of Steyermark.

TO A BAVARIAN GIRL.

Thou, Bavaria's brown-eyed daughter,
Art a shape of joy,
Standing by the Isar's water
With thy brother-boy;
In thy dream, with idle fingers
Threading through his curls,
On thy cheek the sun's kiss lingers,
Rosiest of girls!

Woods of glossy oak are ringing
With the echoes bland,
While thy generous voice is singing
Songs of Fatherland —
Songs, that by the Danube's river
Sound on hills of vine,
And where waves in green light quiver,
Down the rushing Rhine.

Life, with all its hues and changes,
    To thy heart doth lie
Like those dreamy Alpine ranges
    In the southern sky;
Where in haze the clefts are hidden,
    Which the foot should fear,
And the crags that fall unbidden
    Startle not the ear.

Where the village maidens gather
    At the fountain's brim,
Or in sunny harvest-weather,
    With the reapers trim;
Where the autumn fires are burning
    On the vintage-hills;
Where the mossy wheels are turning
    In the ancient mills;

Where from ruined robber-towers
    Hangs the ivy's hair,
And the crimson foxbell flowers
    On the crumbling stair: —
Every where, without thy presence,
    Would the sunshine fail,
Fairest of the maiden peasants!
    Flower of Isar's vale!

MUNICH, 1845.

IN ITALY.

Dear Lillian, all I wished is won!
I sit beneath Italia's sun,
Where olive orchards gleam and quiver
Along the banks of Arno's river.

Through laurel leaves, the dim green light
Falls on my forehead as I write,
And the sweet chimes of vesper, ringing,
Blend with the contadina's singing.

Rich is the soil with Fancy's gold;
The stirring memories of old
Rise thronging in my haunted vision,
And wake my spirit's young ambition.

But as the radiant sunsets close
Above Val d'Arno's bowers of rose,
My soul forgets the olden glory,
And deems our love a dearer story.

Thy words, in Memory's ear, outchime
The music of the Tuscan rhyme;
Thou standest here — the gentle-hearted —
Amid the shades of bards departed.

I see before thee fade away
Their garlands of immortal bay,
And turn from Petrarch's passion-glances
To my own dearer heart-romances.

Sad is the opal glow that fires
The midnight of the cypress spires,
And cold the scented wind that closes
The heart of bright Etruscan roses.

A single thought of thee effaced
The fair Italian dream I chased;
For the true clime of song and sun
Lies in the heart which mine hath won!

FLORENCE, 1845.

THE STATUE IN THE SNOW.

NUMB and chill the Savoyard wandered
  By the banks of frozen Seine,
Oft, to cheer his sinking spirit,
  Singing low some mountain strain.

But, beside the wintry river,
  Rose the songs of green Savoy
Sadder than on Alpine summits,
  Sung by many a shepherd-boy.

From the bleak and distant Jura
  Swept the snowy whirlwind down,
Flinging wide his shifting mantle
  Over slope and meadow brown.

Like a corpse the silent landscape
  Lay all stark and icy there,
And a chill and ghostly terror
  Seemed to load the leaden air.

Still that shivering boy went forward,
  Though his heart within him died,
When the dreary night was closing
  Dull around the desert wide.

Through the desolate northern twilight,
  To his homesick pining, rose
Visions of the flashing glaciers,
  Lifted in sublime repose.

Horns of Alp-herds rang in welcome,
  And his mother kissed her boy —
But away his heart was hurried
  From the vales of dear Savoy!

For, amid the sinking darkness,
  Colder, chillier, blew the snows,
Till but faint and moaning whispers
  From his stiffening lips arose.

Then, beside the pathway kneeling,
  Folded he his freezing hands,
While the blinding snows were drifted
  Like the desert's liftèd sands.

As in many an old cathedral,
  Curtained round with solemn gloom,
One may see a marble cherub
  Kneeling on a marble tomb.

With his face to Heaven upturning,
  For the dead he seems to pray,
While the organ o'er him thunders,
  And the incense curls away.

Thus the Savoyard, pale and lifeless,
  Knelt in Night's cathedral vast,
When the stars at midnight sparkled
  In the pauses of the blast.

PARIS, 1846.

THE DEAREST IMAGE.

I.

I'VE wandered through the golden lands
 Where Art and Beauty blended shine —
Where features limned by painters' hands
 Beam from the canvas made divine,
And many a god in marble stands,
 With soul in every breathing line;
And forms the world has treasured long
Within me touched the source of Song.

II.

Like madness o'er the spirit came
 The boundless rapture they inspired,
As with my feelings all on flame
 I worshipped what the world admired,

While flashes from those orbs of fame
  The soul with mutual ardor fired,
Till Beauty's smile and Glory's star
Seemed to its grasp no more afar.

III.

Yet, brighter than those radiant dreams
  Which won renown that never dies —
Where more than mortal beauty beams
  In sibyls' lips and angels' eyes —
One image, like the moonlight, seems
  Between them and my heart to rise,
And in its brighter, dearer ray,
The stars of Genius fade away.

LONDON, 1846.

A BACCHIC ODE.

WINE — bring wine !
Let the crystal beaker flame and shine,
Brimming o'er with the draught divine !

The crimson glow
Of the lifted cup on my forehead throw,
Like the sunset's flush on a field of snow.

I burn to lave
My thirsty lip in the ruddy wave ;
Freedom bringeth the wine so brave !

The world is cold :
Sorrow and pain have gloomy hold,
Chilling the bosom warm and bold.

Doubts and fears
Veil the shine of my morning years —
My life's lone rainbow springs from tears.

But Eden-gleams
Visit my soul in immortal dreams,
When the wave of the goblet burns and beams.

Not from the Rhine,
Not from fields of Burgundian vine,
Bring me the bright Olympian wine!

Not with a ray
Born where the winds of Shiraz play,
Or the fiery blood of the ripe Tokay.

Not where the glee
Of Falernian vintage echoes free,
Or the Chian gardens gem the sea.

But wine — bring wine,
Royally flushed with its growth divine,
In the crystal depth of my soul to shine!

Whose glow was caught
From the warmth which Fancy's summer brought
To the vintage-fields in the Land of Thought.

Rich and free
To my thirsting soul will the goblet be,
Poured by the Hebe, Poesy.

A FUNERAL THOUGHT.

I.

When the pale Genius, to whose hollow tramp
  Echo the startled chambers of the soul,
Waves his inverted torch o'er that pale camp
  Where the archangel's final trumpets roll,
I would not meet him in the chamber dim,
  Hushed, and pervaded with a nameless fear,
When the breath flutters and the senses swim,
    And the dread hour is near.

II.

Though Love's dear arms might clasp me fondly then,
  As if to keep the Summoner at bay,
And woman's woe and the calm grief of men
  Hallow at last the chill, unbreathing clay —

These are Earth's fetters, and the soul would shrink,
Thus bound, from Darkness and the dread Unknown,
Stretching its arms from Death's eternal brink,
Which it must dare alone.

III.

But in the awful silence of the sky,
Upon some mountain summit, yet untrod,
Through the blue ether would I climb, to die
Afar from mortals and alone with God!
To the pure keeping of the stainless air
Would I resign my faint and fluttering breath,
And with the rapture of an answered prayer
Receive the kiss of Death.

IV.

Then to the elements my frame would turn;
No worms should riot on my coffined clay,
But the cold limbs, from that sepulchral urn,
In the slow storms of ages waste away.

Loud winds and thunder's diapason high
  Should be my requiem through the coming time,
And the white summit, fading in the sky,
    My monument sublime.

THE ANGEL OF THE SOUL.

Una stella, una notte, ed una croce. — Bisazza.

Silence hath conquered thee, imperial Night!
Thou sitt'st alone within her void, cold halls,
Thy solemn brow uplifted, and thy soul
Paining the space with dumb and yearning thought.
The dreary winds are eddying round thy form,
Following the stealthy hours, that wake no stir
In the hushed velvet of thy mantle's fold.
Thy thoughts take being: down the dusky aisles
Glide shapes of good, enticing ghosts of guilt,
And dreams of maddening beauty — hopes, that shine
To darken, and in cloudy height sublime,
The spectral march of some approaching doom.
Nor these alone, O Mother of the world!
People thy chambers, echoless and vast:

Their dewy freshness like ambrosia cools
Life's fever-thirst, and to the fainting soul
Their porphyry walls are touched with light, and gleams
Of shining wonder dance along the void,
Like those processions which the traveller's torch
Wakes from the darkness of three thousand years,
In rock-hewn sepulchres of Theban kings.
Prophets, whose brows of pale, unearthly glow
Reflect the twilight of celestial dawns,
And bards, transfigured in immortal song,
Like eager children, kneeling at thy feet,
Unclasp the awful volume of thy lore.

My soul explores thy far, mysterious realms,
Beyond this being's circumscribed domain,
Touches the threshold of supremer life,
And calls through all the spangled deeps of heaven
Its guardian angel, as an orphan calls
His only brother, that in childhood died :

Thy wings waved white across my cradled dreams,
Lost Angel of the Soul ! Thy presence led
The babe's faint gropings through the glimmering dark
And into Being's conscious dawn. Thy hand
Held mine in childhood, and thy cherub's cheek
Caressed, like some familiar playmate's, mine.

Up to that boundary, whence the heart leaps forth
To life, like some young torrent, when the rains
Pour dark and full upon the cloudy hills,
Thy shining steps kept even pace with mine.
Be with me now! O, in the starry hush
Of holy night, restore to me again
The innocence whose loss was loss of thee!
Through the warm gush of unexpected tears
Let me behold thine eyes divine, as stars
Swim through the twilight vapors of the sea!

Not yet hast thou forsaken me. The prayer
Whose crowning fervor lifts my nature up
Midway to God, may still evoke thy form.
Thou hast returned, what time the midnight dew
Clung damp upon my brow, and the broad fields
Stretched far and dim beneath the ghostly moon;
When the dark, awful woods were silent near,
And with imploring hands towards the stars
Clasped in mute yearning, I have questioned Heaven
For the lost language of the book of Life.
In the last undulating, dying strains
Of tender music, I have heard thy voice;
And thou hast cried amid the stormy rush
Of grand orchestral triumph, calling me
Till every chord became a pang, and calling still

Till I could bear no more. I feel the light,
Which is thine atmosphere, around my soul,
When a great sorrow gulfs it from the world.

Come back! come back! my heart grows faint, to know
How thy withdrawing radiance leaves more dim
The twilight borders of the night of Earth.
Now, when the bitter truth is learned; when all
That seemed so high and good, but mocks its seeming;
When the warm dreams of youth come shivering back,
In the cold chambers of the heart to die;
When, with the wrestling years, familiar grows
The merciless hand of Pain, desert me not!
Come with the true heart of the faithful Night,
When I have thrown aside the masking garb
Of the deceitful Day, and lie at rest
On her consoling bosom! From the founts
Of thine exhaustless light, make clear the road
Through toil and darkness, into God's repose!

AN HOUR.

I'VE left the keen, cold winds to blow
  Around the summits bare ;
My sunny pathway to the sea
  Leads downward, green and fair,
Where leaves and blossoms toss and glow
  Amid the southern air.

The fern its fragrant plumage droops
  O'er mosses crisp and gray,
Where on the shaded crags I sit,
  Beside the cataract's spray,
And watch the far-off, shining sails
  Go down the gleaming bay.

I've left the wintry winds of life
  On barren hearts to blow—
The anguish and the gnawing care,
  The torture and the woe!
I sail the sunny sea of dreams
  Where'er its winds may blow.

Away! away! I hear the horn
  Among the hills of Spain:
The old, chivalric glory fires
  Her warrior hearts again:
Ho! how their banners light the morn
  Along Granada's plain!

I hear the hymns of holy faith
  The red Crusaders sang,
And the silver horn of Ronçeval,
  That o'er the tecbir rang,
When prince and kaiser through the fray
  To the dying paladin sprang.

A beam of burning light I hold,
  My good Damascus brand,

And the jet-black charger that I ride
  Was foaled in the Arab land,
And a hundred horsemen, mailed in steel,
  Follow at my command!

Through royal cities goes our march;
  The minster-bells are rung;
The trumpets give a lordly peal,
  The battle-flags are swung,
And lips of lovely ladies praise
  The chieftain, brave and young.

And now, in soft Provençal bowers,
  A minstrel-knight am I:
A gentle bosom on my own
  Throbs back its ecstasy;
A cheek, as fair as the almond flowers,
  Thrills to my lip's reply.

I tread the fanes of wondrous Rome,
  Crowned with immortal bay,
And myriads crowd the Capitol
  To hear my lofty lay,
While, sounding o'er the Tiber's foam,
  Their shoutings peal away.

O, triumph such as this were worth
  The Poet's doom of pain,
Whose hours are brazen on the earth,
  But golden in the brain:
I close the starry Gate of Dreams,
  And walk the dust again.

THE NORSEMAN'S RIDE.

THE frosty fires of Northern starlight
  Gleamed on the glittering snow,
And through the forest's frozen branches
  The shrieking winds did blow;
A floor of blue, translucent marble
  Kept ocean's pulses still,
When, in the depth of dreary midnight,
  Opened the burial hill.

Then while a low and creeping shudder
  Thrilled upward through the ground,
The Norseman came, as armed for battle,
  In silence from his mound:
He, who was mourned in solemn sorrow
  By many a swordsman bold,
And harps that wailed along the ocean,
  Struck by the Skalds of old.

Sudden, a swift and silver shadow
  Rushed up from out the gloom —
A horse that stamped with hoof impatient,
  Yet noiseless, on the tomb.
" Ha, Surtur! let me hear thy tramping,
  Thou noblest Northern steed,
Whose neigh along the stormy headlands
  Bade the bold Viking heed!"

He mounted: like a north-light streaking
  The sky with flaming bars,
They, on the winds so wildly shrieking,
  Shot up before the stars.
" Is this thy mane, my fearless Surtur,
  That streams against my breast?
Is this thy neck, that curve of moonlight,
  Which Helva's hand caressed?

" No misty breathing strains thy nostril,
  Thine eye shines blue and cold,
Yet, mounting up our airy pathway,
  I see thy hoofs of gold!
Not lighter o'er the springing rainbow
  Walhalla's gods repair,
Than we, in sweeping journey over
  The bending bridge of air.

"Far, far around, star-gleams are sparkling
 Amid the twilight space ;
And Earth, that lay so cold and darkling,
 Has veiled her dusky face.
Are those the Nornes that beckon onward
 To seats at Odin's board,
Where nightly by the hands of heroes
 The foaming mead is poured ?

"'Tis Skuld ! her star-eye speaks the glory
 That waits the warrior's soul,
When on its hinge of music opens
 The gateway of the Pole —
When Odin's warder leads the here
 To banquets never done,
And Freya's eyes outshine in summer
 The ever-risen sun.

"On ! on ! the Northern lights are streaming
 In brightness like the morn,
And pealing far amid the vastness,
 I hear the Gjallarhorn :
The heart of starry space is throbbing
 With songs of minstrels old,
And now, on high Walhalla's portal,
 Gleam Surtur's hoofs of gold !"

THE VOICE OF THE FIRE.

They sat by the hearth-stone, broad and bright,
Whose burning brands threw a cheerful light
On the frosty calm of the winter's night.

Her tresses soft to his lips were pressed,
Her head was laid on his happy breast,
And a tender silence their love expressed :

And ever a gentle murmur came
From the clear, bright heart of the wavering flame,
Like the first sweet call of the dearest name.

He kissed on the warm, white brow,
And told her in fonder words, the vow
He had whispered under the moonlit bough ;

And o'er them a steady radiance came
From the shining heart of the mounting flame,
Like the love that burneth forever the same.

The maiden smiled through her soft brown eyes,
As he led her forward to sunnier skies,
Whose cloudless light on the Future lies ;

And a moment paused the laughing flame,
And it listened a while, and then there came
A cheery burst from its sparkling frame.

In the home he pictured, the home so blest,
Their souls should sit in a calmer rest,
Like woodland birds in their shaded nest.

There slept, foreshadowed, the bliss to be,
When a tenderer life that home should see,
In the wingless cherub that climbed his knee.

And the flame went on with its flickering song,
And beckoned and laughed to the lovers long,
Who sat in its radiance, red and strong.

And ever its burden seemed to be
The mingled voices of household glee,
Like the gush of winds in a mountain tree.

Then broke and fell a glimmering brand
To the cold, dead ashes it fed and fanned,
And its last gleam waved like a warning hand.

They did not speak, for there came a fear,
As a spirit of evil were wandering near,
A menace of danger to something dear.

And, hovering over its smouldering bed,
A feebler pinion the flame outspread,
And a paler light through the chamber shed.

He clasped the maid in a fonder thrall:
" We shall love each other, whatever befall,
And the Merciful Father is over all."

A REQUIEM IN THE NORTH.

SPEED swifter, Night! — wild Northern Night,
  Whose feet the Arctic islands know,
When stiffening breakers, sharp and white,
  Gird the complaining shores of snow!
Send all thy winds to sweep the wold,
  And howl in mountain passes far,
And hang thy banners, red and cold,
  Against the shield of every star!

For what have I to do with morn,
  Or summer's glory in the vales —
With the blithe ring of forest-horn,
  Or beckoning gleam of snowy sails?
Art *thou* not gone, in whose blue eye
  The fleeting summer dawned to me?
Gone, like the echo of a sigh
  Beside the loud, resounding sea!

O, brief that time of song and flowers,
  Which blessed, through thee, the Northern Land ;
I pine amid its leafless bowers,
  And on the bleak and lonely strand.
The forest wails the starry bloom
  Which yet shall light its dusky floor,
But down my spirit's paths of gloom
  Thy love shall blossom nevermore.

And nevermore shall battling pines
  Their solemn triumph sound for me ;
Nor morning gild the mountain lines,
  Nor sunset flush the hoary sea ;
But Night and Winter fill the sky,
  And load with frost the shivering air,
Till every gust that hurries by
  Repeats the tale of my despair.

The leaden twilight, cold and long,
  Is slowly settling o'er the wave ;
No wandering blast awakes a song
  In naked boughs, above thy grave.
The frozen air is still and dark ;
  The numb earth lies in icy rest ;
And all is dead save this one spark
  Of burning grief, within my breast.

Life's darkened orb shall wheel no more
  To Love's rejoicing summer back :
My spirit walks a wintry shore,
  With not a star to cheer its track.
Speed swifter, Night! thy gloom and frost
  Are free to spoil and ravage here ;
This last wild requiem for the lost
  I pour in thy unheeding ear!

A VOICE FROM PIEDMONT.

Avenge, O Lord, Thy slaughtered saints, whose bones
Lie scattered on the Alpine Mountains cold.
MILTON — *Sonnet on the Massacres in Piedmont.*

I.

BEND from that Heaven, whose visioned glories gave,
Thou blind old Bard, the splendor of thy song,
And teach the godlike words which mortals crave,
To speak, exulting, o'er the fallen Wrong!
For lo! the Avenger of that hour of blood
Has heard at last thy summons, stern and grand;
Has freed the children of the slaughtered brood,
In the cold Alpine land!

II.

O! at the tardy word, whose thunder broke
The chains of ages from that suffering flock,

Methinks the mountain's giant soul awoke,
  And thrilled beneath the eternal ribs of rock.
The ancient glaciers brightened in the sky;
  Beneath them, shouting, burst the joyous rills,
And the white Alps of Piedmont made reply
  Unto the Vaudois hills!

III.

And far below, in lonely pasture-vales,
  The Waldense shepherd knelt upon the sod,
While chapel-bells chimed on the mountain gales,
  And every châlet gave its hymn to God.
Matron, and sire, and sweet-voiced peasant maid,
  And the strong hunter from the steeps of snow,
Gave thanks to Him, whose help their fathers prayed,
  Through years of blood and woe.

IV.

Build now the sepulchres of martyrs old:
  Gather the scattered bones from every glen,
Where the red waves of pitiless slaughter rolled,
  When fell those brave and steadfast-hearted men!

Piedmont is free ! and brightening with the years,
Shall Freedom's sun upon her mountains shine ;
While her glad children say, with grateful tears,
"The glory, Lord, be Thine !"

1848.

THE CONTINENTS.

I HAD a vision in that solemn hour,
Last of the year sublime,
Whose wave sweeps downward, with its dying power
Rippling the shores of Time.
On the bleak margin of that hoary sea
My spirit stood alone,
Watching the gleams of phantom History,
Which through the darkness shone.

Then, when the bell of midnight ghostly hands
Tolled for the dead year's doom,
I saw the spirits of Earth's ancient lands
Stand up amid the gloom!
The crownèd deities, whose reign began
In the forgotten Past,
When first the fresh world gave to sovereign Man
Her empires green and vast.

First queenly Asia, from the fallen thrones
Of twice three thousand years,
Came with the woe a grieving goddess owns,
Who longs for mortal tears.
The dust of ruin to her mantle clung
And dimmed her crown of gold,
While the majestic sorrows of her tongue
From Tyre to Indus rolled :

"Mourn with me, sisters, in my realm of woe,
Whose only glory streams
From its lost childhood, like the arctic glow
Which sunless Winter dreams !
In the red desert moulders Babylon,
And the wild serpent's hiss
Echoes in Petra's palaces of stone,
And waste Persepolis.

"Gone are the deities that ruled enshrined
In Elephanta's caves,
And Brahma's wailings fill the fragrant wind
That ripples Ganges' waves :
The ancient gods amid their temples fall,
And shapes of some near doom,
Trembling and waving on the Future's wall,
More fearful make my gloom !"

Then, from her seat, amid the palms embowered
That shade the lion-land,
Swart AFRICA in dusky aspect towered,
The fetters on her hand!
Backward she saw, from out her drear eclipse,
The mighty Theban years,
And the deep anguish of her mournful lips
Interpreted her tears.

"Woe for my children, whom your gyves have bound
Through centuries of toil;
The bitter wailings of whose bondage sound
From many an alien soil!
Leave me but free, though the eternal sand
Be all my kingdom now—
Though the rude splendors of barbaric land
But mock my crownless brow!"

There was a sound, like sudden trumpets blown,
A ringing, as of arms,
When EUROPE rose, a stately amazon,
Stern in her mailèd charms.
She brooded long beneath the weary bars
That chafed her soul of flame,
And like a seer, who reads the awful stars,
Her words prophetic came:

"I hear new sounds along the ancient shore,
Whose dull old monotone
Of tides, that broke on many a system hoar,
Moaned through the ages lone:
I see a gleaming, like the crimson morn
Beneath a stormy sky,
And warning throes, which long my breast has borne,
Proclaim the struggle nigh."

O radiant-browed, the latest born of Time!
How waned thy sisters old,
Before the splendors of thine eye sublime,
And mien erect and bold!
Free, as the winds of thine own forests are,
Thy brow beamed lofty cheer,
And Day's bright oriflamme, the Morning Star,
Flashed on thy lifted spear.

"I bear no weight"—rang thine exulting tones—
"Of memories weird and vast;
No crushing heritage of iron thrones,
Bequeathed by some dead Past;
But hopes, that give my children power to climb
Above the old-world fears—
Whose prophecies forerun the latest time,
And lead the crowning years!

" Like spectral lamps, that burn before a tomb,
The ancient lights expire ;
I hold a torch, that floods the fading gloom
With everlasting fire :
Crowned with my constellated stars, I stand
Beside the foaming sea,
And from the Future, with a victor's hand,
Claim empire for the Free ! "

January, 1848.

THE MOUNTAINS.

O DEEP, exulting freedom of the hills!
  O summits vast, that to the climbing view
  In naked glory stand against the blue!
O cold and buoyant air, whose crystal fills
Heaven's amethystine bowl! O speeding streams,
  That foam and thunder from the cliffs below!
  O slippery brinks and solitudes of snow,
And granite bleakness, where the vulture screams!
O stormy pines, that wrestle with the breath
  Of every tempest, sharp and icy horns,
  And hoary glaciers, sparkling in the morns,
And broad, dim wonders of the world beneath!
I summon ye, and 'mid the glare which fills
The noisy mart, my spirit walks the hills.

LIFE.

O Life ! O Life ! art thou a mocking cheat,
That, with thy flush and fervor in my blood,
Teachest my heart a high, heroic mood,
And passion-joy in all things fair and fleet ?
I know the trumpet winds will join no more
With the high stars and billowed sea, to lift
My spirit to the bard's immortal gift —
That when a few warm summers shall be o'er,
And thy last vintage pours its scanty wine,
All these quick flames will die in ashes low,
The sluggish pulse forget its leaping flow,
And faded lie the flowers of Love divine :
When these, thy bounties, fail to warm my breath,
Leave me, false Life, and send thy brother, Death !

L'ENVOI.

I'VE passed the grim and threatening warders
  That guard the vestibule of Song,
And traced the print of bolder footsteps
  The lengthened corridors along;
Where every thought I strove to blazon
  Beside the bannered lays of old,
Was dim below some bright escutcheon,
  Or shaded by some grander fold.

I saw, in veiled and shadowy glimpses,
  The solemn halls expand afar,
And through the twilight, half despairing,
  Looked trembling up to find a star;
Till, in the rush of wings, awakened
  My soul to utterance free and strong,
And with impassioned exultation,
  I revelled in the rage of Song!

Then, though the world beside, unheeding,
  Heard other voices than my own,
Thou, thou didst mark the broken music,
  And cheer its proud, aspiring tone:
Thou cam'st in many a lovely vision
  To lead my ardent spirit on,
Thine eye my morning-star of promise,
  The sweet anticipant of dawn.

And if I look to holier altars,
  Thou still art near me, as of old,
And thou wilt give the living laurel,
  When the shrined Presence I behold.
Take, then, these echoes of thy being,
  My lips have weakly striven to frame;
For when I speak what thou inspirest,
  I know my songs are nearest fame.

LATER POEMS.

WIND AND SEA.

I.

The Sea is a jovial comrade,
He laughs wherever he goes;
His merriment shines in the dimpling lines
That wrinkle his hale repose;
He lays himself down at the feet of the Sun,
And shakes all over with glee,
And the broad-backed billows fall faint on the shore,
In the mirth of the mighty Sea!

II.

But the Wind is sad and restless,
And cursed with an inward pain;

You may hark as you will, by valley or hill,
  But you hear him still complain.
He wails on the barren mountains,
  And shrieks on the wintry sea;
He sobs in the cedar, and moans in the pine,
  And shudders all over the aspen tree.

III.

Welcome are both their voices,
  And I know not which is best—
The laughter that slips from the Ocean's lips,
  Or the comfortless Wind's unrest.
There's a pang in all rejoicing,
  A joy in the heart of pain,
And the Wind that saddens, the Sea that gladdens,
  Are singing the self-same strain!

MY DEAD.

Give back the soul of Youth once more!
 The years are fleeting fast away,
 And this brown hair will soon be gray,
These cheeks be pale and furrowed o'er.

Ah, no! the child is long since dead,
 Whose light feet spurred the laggard years,
 Who breathed in future atmospheres,
Ere Youth's eternal Present fled.

Dead lies the boy, whose timid eye
 Shunned every face that spake not love;
 Whose simple vision looked above,
And saw a glory in the sky.

And now the youth has sighed his last;
  I see him cold upon his bier,
  But in these eyes there is no tear:
He joins his brethren of the Past.

'Twas time he died: the gates of Art
  Had shut him from the temple's shrine,
  And now I climb her mount divine,
But with the sinews, not the heart.

How many more, O Life! shall I
  In future offer up to thee?
  And shall they perish utterly,
Upon whose graves I clomb so high?

Say, shall I not at last attain
  Some height, from whence the Past is clear,
  In whose immortal atmosphere
I shall behold my Dead again?

THE LOST CROWN.

You ask me why I sometimes drop
  The threads of talk I weave with you,
And midway in expression stop
  As if a sudden trumpet blew.

It is because a trumpet blows
  From steeps your feet will never climb:
It calls my soul from present woes
  To rule some buried realm of Time.

Wide open swing the guarded gates,
  That shut from you the vales of dawn;
And there my car of triumph waits,
  By white, immortal horses drawn.

A throne of gold the wheels uphold,
  Each spoke a ray of jewelled fire:
The crimson banners float unrolled,
  Or falter when the winds expire.

Lo! where the valley's bed expands,
  Through cloudy censer-smoke, upcurled—
The avenue to distant lands—
  The single landscape of a world!

I mount the throne; I seize the rein;
  Between the shouting throngs I go,
The millions crowding hill and plain,
  And now a thousand trumpets blow!

The armies of the world are there,
  The pomp, the beauty, and the power,
Far-shining through the dazzled air,
  To crown the triumph of the hour.

Enthroned aloft, I seem to float
  On wide, victorious wings upborne,
Past the rich vale's expanding throat,
  To where the palace burns with morn.

My limbs dilate, my breast expands,
  A starry fire is in mine eye;
I ride above the subject lands,
  A god beneath the hollow sky.

Peal out, ye clarions! shout, ye throngs,
  Beneath your banners' reeling folds!
This pageantry to me belongs —
  My hand its proper sceptre holds.

Surge on, in still augmenting lines,
  Till the great plain be overrun,
And my procession far outshines
  The bended pathway of the sun!

But when my triumph overtops
  This language, which from vassals grew,
The crown from off my forehead drops,
  And I again am serf with you.

STUDIES FOR PICTURES.

I.

AT HOME.

THE rain is sobbing on the wold;
The house is dark, the hearth is cold;
And stretching drear and ashy gray
Beyond the cedars, lies the bay.

The winds are moaning, as they pass
Through tangled knots of autumn grass —
A weary, dreary sound of woe,
As if all joy were dead below.

I sit alone, I wait in vain
Some voice to lull this nameless pain;
But from my neighbor's cottage near
Come sounds of happy household cheer.

My neighbor at his window stands,
His youngest baby in his hands;
The others seek his tender kiss,
And one sweet woman crowns his bliss.

I look upon the rainy wild:
I have no wife, I have no child:
There is no fire upon my hearth,
And none to love me on the earth.

II.

THE NEIGHBOR.

How cool and wet the lowlands lie
Beneath the cloaked and hooded sky!
How softly beats the welcome rain
Against the plashy window-pane!

There is no sail upon the bay:
We cannot go abroad to-day,
But, darlings, come and take my hand,
And hear a tale of Fairy-land.

The baby's little head shall rest
In quiet on his father's breast,
And mother, if he chance to stir,
Shall sing him songs once sung to her.

Ah, little ones, ye do not fret,
Because the garden grass is wet;
Ye love the rains, whene'er they come,
That all day keep your father home.

No fish to-day the net shall yield;
The happy oxen graze afield;
The thirsty corn will drink its fill,
And louder sing the woodland rill.

Then, darlings, nestle round the hearth;
Ye are the sunshine of the earth:
Your tender eyes so fondly shine,
They bring a welcome rain to mine.

III.

UNDER THE STARS.

How the hot revel's fever dies,
Beneath the stillness of the skies!
How suddenly the whirl and glare
Shoot far away, and this cold air
Its icy beverage brings, to chase
The burning wine-flush from my face!
The window's gleam still faintly falls,
And music sounds at intervals,
Jarring the pulses of the night
With whispers of profane delight;
But on the midnight's awful strand,
Like some wrecked swimmer flung to land,
I lie, and hear those breakers roar:
And smile — they cannot harm me more!

Keep, keep your lamps; they do not mar
The silver of a single star.
The painted roses you display
Drop from your cheeks, and fade away;

The snowy warmth you bid me see
Is hollowness and mockery;
The words that make your sin so fair
Grow silent in this vestal air;
The loosened madness of your hair,
That wrapped me in its snaky coils,
No more shall mesh me in your toils;
Your very kisses on my brow
Burn like the lips of devils now.
O sacred night! O virgin calm!
Teach me the immemorial psalm
Of your eternal watch sublime
Above the grovelling lusts of Time!
Within, the orgie shouts and reels;
Without, the planets' golden wheels
Spin, circling through the utmost space;
Within, each flushed and reckless face
Is masked to cheat a haunting care;
Without, the silence and the prayer.
Within, the beast of flesh controls;
Without, the God that speaks in souls!

IV.

IN THE MORNING.

The lamps were thick; the air was hot;
The heavy curtains hushed the room;
The sultry midnight seemed to blot
All life but ours in vacant gloom.

You spoke: my blood in every vein
Throbbed, as by sudden fever stirred,
And some strange whirling in my brain
Subdued my judgment, as I heard.

Ah, yes! when men are dead asleep,
When all the tongues of Day are still,
The heart must sometimes fail to keep
Its natural poise 'twixt good and ill.

You knew too well its blind desires,
Its savage instincts, scarce confessed;
I could not see you touch the wires,
But felt your lightning in my breast.

For you, Life's web displayed its flaws,
  The wrong which Time transforms to right:
The iron mesh of social laws
  Was but a cobweb in your sight.

You showed that tempting freedom, where
  The passions bear their perfect fruit,
The cheats of conscience cannot scare,
  And Self is monarch absolute.

And something in me seemed to rise,
  And trample old obedience down:
The serf sprang up, with furious eyes,
  And clutched at the imperial crown.

That fierce rebellion overbore
  The arbiter that watched within,
Till Sin so changed an aspect wore,
  It was no longer that of Sin.

You gloried in the fevered flush
  That spread, defiant, o'er my face,
Nor thought how soon this morning's blush
  Would chronicle the night's disgrace.

I wash my eyes; I bathe my brow;
  I see the sun on hill and plain:
The old allegiance claims me now,
  The old content returns again.

Ah, seek to stop the sober glow
  And healthy airs that come with day,
For when the cocks at dawning crow,
  Your evil spirits flee away.

SUNKEN TREASURES.

WHEN the uneasy waves of life subside,
And the soothed ocean sleeps in glassy rest,
I see, submerged beyond or storm or tide,
The treasures gathered in its greedy breast.

There still they shine, through the translucent Past,
Far down on that forever quiet floor;
No fierce upheaval of the deep shall cast
Them back — no wave shall wash them to the shore.

I see them gleaming, beautiful as when
Erewhile they floated, convoys of my fate;
The barks of lovely women, noble men,
Full-sailed with hope, and stored with Love's own freight.

The sunken ventures of my heart as well,
  Look up to me, as perfect as at dawn ;
My golden palace heaves beneath the swell
  To meet my touch, and is again withdrawn.

There sleep the early triumphs, cheaply won,
  That led Ambition to his utmost verge,
And still his visions, like a drowning sun,
  Send up receding splendors through the surge.

There wait the recognitions, the quick ties,
  Whence the heart knows its kin, wherever cast ;
And there the partings, when the wistful eyes
  Caress each other as they look their last.

There lie the summer eves, delicious eves,
  The soft green valleys drenched with light divine,
The lisping murmurs of the chestnut leaves,
  The hand that lay, the eyes that looked in mine.

There lives the hour of fear and rapture yet,
  The perilled climax of the passionate years ;
There still the rains of wan December wet
  A naked mound — I cannot see for tears !

There are they all: they do not fade or waste,
  Lapped in the arms of the embalming brine;
More fair than when their beings mine embraced—
  Of nobler aspect, beauty more divine.

I see them all, but stretch my hands in vain;
  No deep-sea plummet reaches where they rest;
No cunning diver shall descend the main,
  And bring a single jewel from its breast.

A FANTASY.

O MAIDEN of the Forest,
  Why play so loud and long?
Now let thy horn be silent,
  Thy voice take up the song!

I cannot choose but listen,
  I cannot choose but follow,
Where'er thy blue eyes glisten
  Across the woodlands hollow.

My heart is filled with brightness
  As the heavens are filled with morn,
To hear the sounds enchanted
  Leap from thy silver horn.

Let the echoes rest a moment,
  And let thy lips declare
If thou be of earth or ocean,
  Or the flying shapes of air.

Let my mouth be free to kiss thee,
  Let my hands be free to hold,
For I cannot choose but love thee,
  And love is ever bold.

Still she played, and playing, fleeted
  Before me as I sought her,
And the horn rang out this answer
  Across the shaded water :

I play the strains enchanted
  You cannot choose but hear,
For your life is in the music,
  And your heart sits at your ear.

I shall never cease my playing
  For your love's impassioned prayer ;
I shall never feel your kisses
  Falling on my golden hair.

For my touch would chill your pulses,
  And my kiss make dim your eye,
And the horn will first be silent
  In the hour that you shall die.

THE VOYAGERS.

No longer spread the sail!
  No longer strain the oar!
For never yet has blown the gale
  Will bring us nearer shore.

The swaying keel slides on,
  The helm obeys the hand;
Fast we have sailed from dawn to dawn,
  Yet never reach the land.

Each morn we see its peaks,
  Made beautiful with snow;
Each eve its vales and winding creeks,
  That sleep in mist below.

At noon we mark the gleam
  Of temples tall and fair;
At midnight watch its bonfires stream
  In the auroral air.

And still the keel is swift,
  And still the wind is free,
And still as far its mountains lift
  Beyond the enchanted sea.

Yet vain is all return,
  Though false the goal before;
The gale is ever dead astern,
  The current sets to shore.

O shipmates, leave the ropes —
  And what though no one steers,
We sail no faster for our hopes,
  No slower for our fears.

Howe'er the bark is blown,
  Lie down and sleep awhile:
What profits toil, when chance alone
  Can bring us to the isle?

MEMORY.

O give me the tongue of the silver sea,
  Or the flute of the twilight wind,
  For a tenderer music my heart would find,
To sing of the sadness and sweetness of Memory!

Joy is a goblet that soon is drained;
  It cracks in our heedless hands;
  But the cup of Remembrance forever stands,
Filled with libations the wormwood of tears has stained.

We lift it against the dying sun;
  We drink till the eyes run o'er;
  We drink till the heart will contain no more,
And surfeited turns from the Lethe it has not won.

For all can look around and before,
  But few can steadily turn
  Where the unextinguished beacons burn,
Far back on the cliffs of the lost, unreachable shore.

Few can sit at the board of the Past,
  The Barmecide feast of the soul,
  And catch and sing over its songs as they roll,
For the heart-strings attuned to their burthen are
      broken at last.

THE MARINERS.

They were born by the shore, by the shore,
  When the surf was loud and the sea-gull cried ;
They were rocked to the rhythm of its roar,
  They were cradled in the arms of the tide.

Sporting on the fenceless sand,
  Looking o'er the limitless blue,
Half on the water and half on the land,
  Ruddily and lustily to manhood they grew.

How should they follow where the plough
  Furrows at the heels of the lazy steers ?
How should they stand with a sickly brow,
  Pent behind a counter, wasting golden years ?

They turned to the Earth, but she frowns on her child;
  They turned to the Sea, and he smiled as of old;
Sweeter was the peril of the breakers white and wild,
  Sweeter than the land with its bondage and gold!

Now they walk on the rolling deck,
  And they hang to the rocking shrouds,
When the lee-shore looms with a vision of wreck,
  And the scud is flung to the stooping clouds.

Shifting the changeless horizon ring,
  Which the lands and islands in turn look o'er,
They traverse the zones with a veering wing,
  From shore to sea, and from sea to shore.

They know the South and the North;
  They know the East and the West;
Shuttles of fortune, flung back and forth
  In the web of motion, the woof of rest.

They do not act with a studied grace,
  They do not speak in delicate phrase,
But the candor of heaven is on their face,
  And the freedom of ocean in all their ways.

They cannot fathom the subtle cheats,
  The lying arts which the landsmen learn :
Each looks in the eyes of the man he meets,
  And whoso trusts him, he trusts in turn.

Say that they curse, if you will,
  That the tavern and harlot possess their gains :
On the surface floats what they do of ill —
  At the bottom the manhood remains.

When they slide from the gangway-plank below,
  Deep as the plummeted shroud may drag,
They hold it comfort enough, to know
  The corpse is wrapped in their country's flag.

But whether they die on the sea or shore,
  And lie under water, or sand, or sod,
Christ give them the rest that he keeps in store,
  And anchor their souls in the harbors of God !

NOTE.

Mon-da-Min; or, the Romance of Maize. — For the Indian legend embodied in this poem, the author is indebted to the very curious and valuable "Algic Researches" of Mr. Schoolcraft. He has added nothing to the simple and beautiful story of the Origin of Maize, as there related, — a story which charmed him the more, from its unexpected grace and symmetry, in the midst of so many grotesque and exaggerated forms of tradition.

BOSTON, 135 WASHINGTON STREET,
NOVEMBER, 1855.

NEW BOOKS AND NEW EDITIONS
PUBLISHED BY
TICKNOR AND FIELDS.

CHARLES READE.

PEG WOFFINGTON. A NOVEL. Price 75 cents.
CHRISTIE JOHNSTONE. A NOVEL. Price 75 cents.
CLOUDS AND SUNSHINE. A NOVEL. Price 75 cents.
SUSAN MERTON. A NOVEL. (Nearly ready).

WILLIAM HOWITT.

LAND, LABOR AND GOLD. 2 vols. Price $2.00
A BOY'S ADVENTURES IN AUSTRALIA. Price 75 cents.

THOMAS DE QUINCEY'S WRITINGS.

CONFESSIONS OF AN ENGLISH OPIUM-EATER, AND SUSPIRIA DE PROFUNDIS. With Portrait. Price 75 cents.
BIOGRAPHICAL ESSAYS. Price 75 cents.
MISCELLANEOUS ESSAYS. Price 75 cents.
THE CÆSARS. Price 75 cents.
LITERARY REMINISCENCES. 2 Vols. Price $1.50.
NARRATIVE AND MISCELLANEOUS PAPERS. 2 Vols. Price $1.50.
ESSAYS ON THE POETS, &c. 1 vol. 16mo. 75 cents.
HISTORICAL AND CRITICAL ESSAYS. 2 vols. $1.50.
AUTOBIOGRAPHIC SKETCHES. 1 vol. Price 75 cents.
ESSAYS ON PHILOSOPHICAL WRITERS, &c. 2 vols. 16mo. $1.50.
LETTERS TO A YOUNG MAN, AND OTHER PAPERS. 1 vol. Price 75 cents.
THEOLOGICAL ESSAYS AND OTHER PAPERS. 2 Vols. Price $1.50.
THE NOTE BOOK. 1 vol. Price 75 cents.

HENRY W. LONGFELLOW'S WRITINGS.

THE SONG OF HIAWATHA. Price $1.00.

THE GOLDEN LEGEND. A Poom. Price $1.00.

POETICAL WORKS. This edition contains the six Volumes mentioned below. In two volumes. 16mo. Boards $2.00.

In Separate Volumes, each 75 cents.

VOICES OF THE NIGHT.
BALLADS AND OTHER POEMS.
SPANISH STUDENT; A PLAY IN THREE ACTS.
BELFRY OF BRUGES, AND OTHER POEMS.
EVANGELINE; A TALE OF ACADIE.
THE SEASIDE AND THE FIRESIDE.
THE WAIF. A Collection of Poems. Edited by Longfellow.
THE ESTRAY. A Collection of Poems. Edited by Longfellow.

MR. LONGFELLOW'S PROSE WORKS.

HYPERION. A ROMANCE. Price $1.00.
OUTRE-MER. A PILGRIMAGE. Price $1.00.
KAVANAGH. A TALE. Price 75 cents.

Illustrated editions of EVANGELINE, POEMS, HYPERION, and THE GOLDEN LEGEND.

ALFRED TENNYSON'S WRITINGS.

POETICAL WORKS. With Portrait. 2 vols. Cloth. $1.50.

THE PRINCESS. Cloth. Price 50 cents.

IN MEMORIAM. Cloth. Price 75 cents.

MAUD, AND OTHER POEMS. Cloth. Price 50 cents.

OLIVER WENDELL HOLMES'S WRITINGS.

POETICAL WORKS. With fine Portrait. Boards. $1.00.

ASTRÆA. Fancy paper. Price 25 cents.

NATHANIEL HAWTHORNE'S WRITINGS.

TWICE-TOLD TALES. Two Volumes. Price $1.50.

THE SCARLET LETTER. Price 75 cents.

THE HOUSE OF THE SEVEN GABLES. Price $1.00.

THE SNOW IMAGE, AND OTHER TWICE-TOLD TALES. Price 75 cents.

THE BLITHEDALE ROMANCE. Price 75 cents.

MOSSES FROM AN OLD MANSE. New Edition. 2 vols. Price $1.50.

TRUE STORIES FROM HISTORY AND BIOGRAPHY. With four fine Engravings. Price 75 cents.

A WONDER-BOOK FOR GIRLS AND BOYS. With seven fine Engravings. Price 75 cents.

TANGLEWOOD TALES. Another 'Wonder-Book.' With Engravings. Price 88 cents.

BARRY CORNWALL'S WRITINGS.

ENGLISH SONGS AND OTHER SMALL POEMS. Enlarged Edition. Price $1.00.

ESSAYS AND TALES IN PROSE. 2 Vols. Price $1.50.

JAMES RUSSELL LOWELL'S WRITINGS.

COMPLETE POETICAL WORKS. Revised, with Additions. In two volumes, 16mo. Cloth. Price $1.50.

SIR LAUNFAL. New Edition. Price 25 cents.

A FABLE FOR CRITICS. New Edition. Price 50 cents.

THE BIGLOW PAPERS. A New Edition. Price 63 cents.

CHARLES KINGSLEY.

AMYAS LEIGH. A Novel. Price $1.25.

GLAUCUS; OR, THE WONDERS OF THE SHORE. 50 cents.

POETICAL WORKS. (In Press.)

A CHRISTMAS BOOK. (In Press.)

CHARLES SUMNER.

ORATIONS AND SPEECHES. 2 vols. $2.50.

A NEW VOLUME. (In Press.)

JOHN G. WHITTIER'S WRITINGS.

OLD PORTRAITS AND MODERN SKETCHES. 75 cents.

MARGARET SMITH'S JOURNAL. Price 75 cents.

SONGS OF LABOR, AND OTHER POEMS. Boards. 50 cts.

THE CHAPEL OF THE HERMITS. Cloth. 50 cents.

LITERARY RECREATIONS AND MISCELLANIES. Cloth. $1.00.

EDWIN P. WHIPPLE'S WRITINGS.

ESSAYS AND REVIEWS. 2 Vols. Price $2.00.

LECTURES ON SUBJECTS CONNECTED WITH LITERATURE AND LIFE. Price 63 cents.

WASHINGTON AND THE REVOLUTION. Price 20 cts.

GEORGE S. HILLARD'S WRITINGS.

SIX MONTHS IN ITALY. 1 vol. 16mo. Price $1.50.

DANGERS AND DUTIES OF THE MERCANTILE PROFESSION. Price 25 cents.

WISDOM AND GENIUS OF WALTER SAVAGE LANDOR.

HENRY GILES'S WRITINGS.

LECTURES, ESSAYS, AND MISCELLANEOUS WRITINGS. 2 Vols. Price $1.50.

DISCOURSES ON LIFE. Price 75 cents.

ILLUSTRATIONS OF GENIUS. Cloth. $1.00.

BAYARD TAYLOR'S WRITINGS.

POEMS OF HOME AND TRAVEL Cloth. Price 75 cents..

POEMS OF THE ORIENT. Cloth. 75 cents.

WILLIAM MOTHERWELL'S WRITINGS.

POEMS, NARRATIVE AND LYRICAL. New Ed. $1.25.

POSTHUMOUS POEMS. Boards. Price 50 cents.

MINSTRELSY, ANC. AND MOD. 2 Vols. Boards. $1.50.

ROBERT BROWNING.

POETICAL WORKS. 2 vols. $2.00.

MEN AND WOMEN. 1 vol. Price $1.00.

CAPT. MAYNE REID'S JUVENILE BOOKS.

THE DESERT HOME, or, The Adventures of a Lost Family in the Wilderness. With fine Plates, $1.00.

THE BOY HUNTERS. With fine Plates. Just published. Price 75 cents.

THE YOUNG VOYAGEURS, or, THE BOY HUNTERS IN THE NORTH. With plates. Price 75 cents.

THE FOREST EXILES. With fine Plates. 75 cents.

GOETHE'S WRITINGS.

WILHELM MEISTER. Translated by THOMAS CARLYLE. 2 Vols. Price $2.50.

GOETHE'S FAUST. Translated by HAYWARD. Price 75 cts.

R. H. STODDARD'S WRITINGS.

POEMS. Cloth. Price 63 cents.

ADVENTURES IN FAIRY LAND. Price 75 cents.

REV. CHARLES LOWELL, D. D.

PRACTICAL SERMONS. 1 vol. 12mo. $1.25.

OCCASIONAL SERMONS. With fine Portrait. $1.25.

GEORGE LUNT.

LYRIC POEMS, &c. Cloth. 63 cents.

JULIA. A Poem. 50 cents.

PHILIP JAMES BAILEY.

THE MYSTIC AND OTHER POEMS. 50 cents.

THE ANGEL WORLD, &c. 50 cents.

ANNA MARY HOWITT.

AN ART STUDENT IN MUNICH. Price $1.25

A SCHOOL OF LIFE. A Story. Price 75 cents.

MARY RUSSELL MITFORD'S WRITINGS.

OUR VILLAGE. Illustrated. 2 Vols. 16mo. Price $2.50.

ATHERTON AND OTHER STORIES. 1 Vol. 16mo. $1.25.

MRS. CROSLAND'S WRITINGS.

LYDIA: A WOMAN'S BOOK. Cloth. Price 75 cents.

ENGLISH TALES AND SKETCHES. Cloth. $1.00.

MEMORABLE WOMEN. Illustrated. $1.00.

GRACE GREENWOOD'S WRITINGS.

GREENWOOD LEAVES. 1st & 2d Series. $1.25 each.

POETICAL WORKS. With fine Portrait. Price 75 cents.

HISTORY OF MY PETS. With six fine Engravings. Scarlet cloth. Price 50 cents.

RECOLLECTIONS OF MY CHILDHOOD. With six fine Engravings. Scarlet cloth. Price 50 cents.

HAPS AND MISHAPS OF A TOUR IN EUROPE. Price $1.25.

MERRIE ENGLAND. A new Juvenile. Price 75 cents.

THE FOREST SISTERS. (In Press.)

A NEW JUVENILE. (In Press.)

MRS. MOWATT.

AUTOBIOGRAPHY OF AN ACTRESS. Price $1.25.

PLAYS. ARMAND AND FASHION. Price 50 cts.

MIMIC LIFE. 1 vol. Price $1.25.

ALICE CARY.

POEMS. 1 vol. 16mo. Price $1.00.

CLOVERNOOK CHILDREN. With Plates. 75 cents.

MRS. TAPPAN.

RAINBOWS FOR CHILDREN. Illustrated. 75 cents.

THE MAGICIAN'S SHOW BOX. Illustrated. 75 cents.

MRS. ELIZA LEE.

MEMOIR OF THE BUCKMINSTERS. $1.25.

FLORENCE, THE PARISH ORPHAN. 50 cents.

MRS. JUDSON'S WRITINGS.

ALDERBROOK. BY FANNY FORRESTER. 2 vols. Price $1.75.

THE KATHAYAN SLAVE, AND OTHER PAPERS. 1 vol. Price 63 cents.

MY TWO SISTERS: A SKETCH FROM MEMORY. Price 50 cts.

POETRY.

ALEXANDER SMITH'S POEMS. 1 Vol. 16mo. Cloth. Price 50 cents.

CHARLES MACKAY'S POEMS. 1 Vol. Cloth. Price $1.00.

HENRY ALFORD'S POEMS. Just out. Price $1.25.

RICHARD MONCKTON MILNES. POEMS OF MANY YEARS. Boards. Price 75 cents.

CHARLES SPRAGUE. Poetical and Prose Writings. With fine Portrait. Boards. Price 75 cents.

GERMAN LYRICS. Translated by Charles T. Brooks. 1 vol. 16mo. Cloth. Price $1.00.

THOMAS W. PARSONS. Poems. Price $1.00.

LYTERIA: A Dramatic Poem. By J. P. Quincy. Price 50 cents.

JOHN G. SAXE. Poems. With Portrait. Boards, 63 cents. Cloth, 75 cents.

HENRY T. TUCKERMAN. Poems. Cloth. Price 75 cents.

BOWRING'S MATINS AND VESPERS. Price 50 cents.

YRIARTE'S FABLES. Translated by G. H. Devereux. Price 63 cents.

MEMORY AND HOPE. A Book of Poems, referring to Childhood. Cloth. Price $2.00.

THALATTA: A Book for the Sea-Side. 1 vol. 16mo. Cloth. Price 75 cts.

PASSION-FLOWERS. By Mrs. Howe. Price 75 cents.

PHŒBE CARY. Poems and Parodies. 75 cents.

MISCELLANEOUS.

G. H. LEWES. The Life and Works of Goethe. 2 vols. 16mo

OAKFIELD. A Novel. By Lieut. Arnold. Price $1.00.

ESSAYS ON THE FORMATION OF OPINIONS AND THE PURSUIT OF TRUTH. 1 vol. 16mo. Price $1.00.

WALDEN: or, LIFE IN THE WOODS. By Henry D. Thoreau. 1 vol. 16mo. Price $1.00.

LIGHT ON THE DARK RIVER: OR, MEMOIRS OF MRS. HAMLIN. 1 vol. 16mo. Cloth. Price $1.00.

WILLIAM MOUNTFORD. THORPE: A QUIET ENGLISH TOWN, AND HUMAN LIFE THEREIN. 16mo. Price $1.00.

NOTES FROM LIFE. BY HENRY TAYLOR, author of 'Philip Van Artevelde.' 1 vol. 16mo. Cloth. Price 63 cents.

REJECTED ADDRESSES. By HORACE and JAMES SMITH. Boards, Price 50 cents. Cloth, 63 cents.

WARRENIANA. A Companion to the 'Rejected Addresses.' Price 63 cents.

WILLIAM WORDSWORTH'S BIOGRAPHY. 2 vols. $2.50.

ART OF PROLONGING LIFE. By HUFELAND. Edited by ERASMUS WILSON, F. R. S. 1 vol. 16mo. Price 75 cents.

JOSEPH T. BUCKINGHAM'S PERSONAL MEMOIRS AND RECOLLECTIONS OF EDITORIAL LIFE. With Portrait. 2 vols. 16mo. Price $1.50.

VILLAGE LIFE IN EGYPT. By the Author of 'Purple Tints of Paris.' 2 vols. 16mo. Price $1.25.

DR. JOHN C. WARREN. THE PRESERVATION OF HEA TH, &c. 1 Vol. Price 38 cents.

PRIOR'S LIFE OF EDMUND BURKE. 2 vols. $2.00.

NATURE IN DISEASE. BY DR. JACOB BIGELOW. 1 vol. 16mo. Price $1.50.

WENSLEY: A STORY WITHOUT A MORAL. Price 75 cts.

GOLDSMITH. THE VICAR OF WAKEFIELD. Illustrated Edition. Price $3.00.

PALISSY THE POTTER. By the Author of 'How to make Home Unhealthy.' 2 vols. 16mo. Price $1.50.

THE BARCLAYS OF BOSTON. BY MRS. H. G. OTIS. 1 vol. 12mo. $1.25.

HORACE MANN. THOUGHTS FOR A YOUNG MAN. 25 cents.

F. W. P. GREENWOOD. SERMONS OF CONSOLATION. $1.00.

THE BOSTON BOOK. Price $1.25.

ANGEL-VOICES. Price 38 cents.

SIR ROGER DE COVERLEY. From the 'Spectator.' 75 cts.

S. T. WALLIS. SPAIN, HER INSTITUTIONS, POLITICS, AND PUBLIC MEN. Price $1.00.

MEMOIR OF ROBERT WHEATON. 1 Vol. Price $1.00.

LABOR AND LOVE: A TALE OF ENGLISH LIFE. 50 cents.

MRS. PUTNAM'S RECEIPT BOOK; AN ASSISTANT TO HOUSEKEEPERS. 1 vol. 16mo. Price 50 cents.

MRS. A. C. LOWELL. EDUCATION OF GIRLS. Price 25 cts.

THE SOLITARY OF JUAN FERNANDEZ. By the Author of Picciola. Price 50 cents.

RUTH. A New Novel by the Author of 'MARY BARTON.' Cheap Edition. Price 38 cents.

EACH OF THE ABOVE POEMS AND PROSE WRITINGS, MAY BE HAD IN VARIOUS STYLES OF HANDSOME BINDING.

☞ Any book published by TICKNOR & FIELDS, will be sent by mail postage free, on receipt of the publication price.

Their stock of Miscellaneous Books is very complete, and they respectfully solicit orders from CITY AND COUNTRY LIBRARIES.

www.ingramcontent.com/pod-product-compliance
Lightning Source LLC
LaVergne TN
LVHW010238110826
845151LV00004B/1328

* 9 7 8 1 4 2 5 5 2 4 1 3 5 *